Aardvark Press
and
Albert J. Thiel
are extremely pleased to
bring you this second printing
of

John H. Tullock's

most popular

The Reef Tank Owner's Manual

Aardvark Press is a division of
Thiel Aqua Tech Inc.

THE REEF TANK

OWNER'S MANUAL

BY

John H. Tullock

August 13, 1992

The Reef Tank Owner's Manual is published by :

Aardvark Press
P.O. Box 1176
Mesilla Park, NM 88047-1176

Telephone : (505) 526 4000
Fax : (505) 524 7313

who also publish :

The Marine Fish and Invert Reef Aquarium, Albert J. Thiel
Small Reef Aquarium Basics, Albert J. Thiel
Advanced Reef Keeping I, Albert J. Thiel
Advanced Reef Keeping II, Albert J. Thiel (publishing date is not set)
10 Easy Steps to a Great Looking Saltwater Aquarium, Albert J. Thiel
The Marine Reef, 34 issues in hardbound format, Albert J. Thiel

The Reef Tank Owner's Manual, © 1992 John H. Tullock
and Aardvark Press

10 9 8 7 6 5 4 3 2

ISBN: 0-945777-06-X

Set in Pagemaker 4.2 from Aldus
using Serifa Roman (Adobe)
on a Powerbook 170 from Apple Computers

The Reef Tank

Owner's Manual

John H. Tullock

Published by :
Aardvark Press
Mesilla Park, New Mexico

DEDICATION

This book is dedicated to:

Jerry, J.R., Martha, Pat, Ken, Don and Randall,
the Staff of Aquatic Specialists;

Albert J. Thiel;
Boyce Phipps;

and the thousands of hobbyists without
whom there would be no reef tanks,
and no need for this book.

Table of Contents

Foreword

John Tullock's "The Reef Tank Owner's Manual"is a book that is so complete and so well structured that no hobbyist purporting to run a balanced reef aquarium, or preparing to set up such a tank, should be without it.

It is both a very practical and comprehensive guide to the animals and invertebrates that can be kept in such aquariums, and a problem solving manual that allows hobbyists to maintain such aquariums without incurring a large initial investment.

It approaches reef keeping from the standpoint of the hobbyist, demonstrates in great detail how all the pieces of the reef keeping puzzle fit together, and does so in language that is easy to understand yet is not simplistic or lacking in detail.

Mr. Tullock has written a book that impressed me a great deal and that has taught me a few things along the way.

It shows respect for the animals kept in reef tanks, and understanding for the hobbyist's predicaments, while offering sensible and easy-to-implement solutions to many problems hobbyists may encounter in the course of keeping a reef tank.

The building block approach will get the hobbyist safely from an empty tank to a complete reef aquarium in a matter of 30 to 40 days.

The book demystifies reef keeping and dispels many misconceptions that may, presently, still exist with regard to the keeping of reef fishes, corals, crustaceans, and so on in a closed environment.

Not only are the filtration, lighting, and water quality parameter aspects well documented and explained, but additionally the book covers many of the animals typically maintained.

It discusses the specific requirements of the animals, something that is lacking in other books now on the market. That particular part of the book alone makes it a good buy. Add to that the sections on filtration, macro and microalgae, and this book becomes a must for any reef hobbyist's library.

The book is replete with suggestions and details that will help beginners, intermediate, and advanced hobbyists alike optimize their reef tanks. Whether you use the book as a manual to set up your captive reef, or whether you use it to freshen up your knowledge of the animals, you will greatly benefit from it.

I strongly recommend "The Reef Tank Owner's Manual" to everyone. It is the best book on reef tanks that I have read in years.

Albert J. Thiel
Publisher and Author
Aardvark Press
Las Cruces, New Mexico

Preface to the Second Printing

Many thanks are due to all of the people who contributed comments and suggestions for improvement to this second edition of "*The Reef Tank Owner's Manual*".

Not the least of these are the many hobbyists who have called or written me to provide additional input.

To all of you who have asked for more pictures and illustrations, we must apologize for the fact that we have not been able to do much to increase the number of illustrations for this edition.

The bright side of this is that we have been able to keep the cost of producing the book low enough to continue to offer it to you at a reasonable price.

I am, however, planning a future volume that I hope will be chock full of photos, especially of invertebrates. Keep those letters and phone calls coming.

Several howling errors found their way into the first edition, for which I apologize to anyone who was misled. For example, the section on *Tridacna* clams has been corrected and expanded. And my awful error in calculating calcium concentrations on page 245 has been corrected, and the section has been expanded somewhat.

Recent changes in our understanding of how marine aquariums operate have been incorporated into the text of this edition.

I have written a whole new chapter, Chapter 15, devoted to two subjects that have recently begun to gain attention. Concern has been raised about the detrimental effects of induced electrical charge in the reef tank.

I discuss the evidence to date and the easy remedy for this problem.

Second, I provide a brief, and I hope tantalizing, introduction to the subject of "low-tech" reef tanks. Sometimes called "natural method" reef tanks, these systems rely on live rock, protein skimming, intense, wide spectrum lighting, and regular supplementation of inorganic ions to achieve spectacular results without the use of wet/dry filters, ozone, controllers, and other, similar technology.

Revising this book has been an odyssey of pleasure for me.

I have learned, more clearly than ever, of the dynamic nature of this hobby. We are always experimenting, always seeking new horizons, always expanding our awareness of the richness of the sea and its many mysteries.

I look forward with excitement to the next twenty years.

John H. Tullock
August 13, 1992
Knoxville, TN

Introduction

Marine aquarium keeping has experienced expanded horizons over the last few years.

The introduction of wet/dry filtration technology, originally borrowed from municipal waste treatment engineering, for the first time made it possible for the average hobbyist to maintain live corals and similar invertebrates in captivity.

Marine tanks have thus become more than mere displays of fishes. We have moved into the realm of creating in the aquarium a tiny segment of coral reef, replete with many of the diverse life forms that inhabit these fantastic underwater jungles.

A proliferation of new technology has accompanied the increased interest in reef aquariums. Much of this new equipment is useful, but some of it contributes little to the overall success of the aquarium. The average hobbyist will have a difficult time distinguishing the difference.

Further complicating matters is the fact that reef life forms available to aquarists come from a variety of geographic locations, and an even wider variety of habitats within a particular reef system.

Dealing with the staggering diversity of both equipment and livestock can be a daunting task. This book was written with the intention of making life easier for the hobbyist who is determined to establish a reef tank, but is unsure as to how to proceed.

There are several points about reef tanks that must be clearly understood from the outset, if there is to be any hope of long term success.

First and foremost, a reef tank requires a substantial commitment of both time and money — but so does any other worthwhile pursuit.

Second, many dealers have been stocking marine fish for years, but most have only recently become familiar with reef tanks.

Much of your personal success will depend upon the quality of both the advice and the animals that you receive from your dealer.

The effort involved in the proper collection, shipment, and holding of live marine organisms entails considerable expense and great risk.

You should expect the services of all the people who have responsibility for these marine organisms between the reef and your reef tank to be appropriately compensated.

By the same token, good quality, reliable equipment will cost more than shoddy equipment, but is worth it in the long run.

With a reef tank, you should be prepared to do it properly, or not at all.

Another important consideration for the would-be reef keeper is the very real requirement to learn about the aquarium system and the animals within it.

You won't need to go to night school for courses in chemistry and marine biology, but you must develop a taste for these subjects and an understanding of the basic principles that apply to the extremely complex ecosystems we call coral reefs.

Many of these same principles apply to reef aquariums as well.

Finally, remember that all of the living organisms that will populate your reef aquarium were collected from natural coral reefs.

In exchange for your enjoyment of their beauty, you should be willing to supply these creatures with conditions that will promote their prosperity in your aquarium. Suppose, for example, that your neighbor acquires a new puppy.

You observe that the dog is kept chained within a tiny, dirty enclosure, is fed and watered indifferently and only occasionally.

Wouldn't you be outraged? Wouldn't you speak to your neighbor, or perhaps to the Humane Society?

If so, why then would one want to acquire an Emperor Angelfish or an Elegance Coral, and then consign such a magnificent creature to a miserable existence and an early death?

One theme that you will find throughout this book is the importance of approaching marine organisms with the respect and consideration for their needs that these animals deserve.

This is the first principle of conservation, and conservation, not only of coral reef organisms, but of all the world's natural resources, is a goal we must all work to promote.

None of the foregoing is meant to dissuade you from owning a reef tank. Aquarium keeping is a rewarding and exciting hobby which has for me provided over 30 years of satisfaction.

Learning the art and science of reef tank keeping is no more challenging than learning gourmet cooking, or golf, or any of a thousand other pursuits that one might choose for a leisure time activity.

But, just like the chef or the golf pro, one is not born knowing how to maintain a reef tank successfully.

One must learn from others as well as acquire practical experience on one's own. This book is a place to begin that learning process.

Once begun, the learning process continues, as you will delight in new discoveries every day that you own a reef tank. The organisms that live on coral reefs are exquisitely adapted to their special lifestyles.

To our great good fortune as observant humans, most of these organisms will exhibit their special traits in the captive environment of the aquarium, and one never knows when one will encounter some new trait or behavior in a captive specimen that no one else has ever seen or written about.

I have spent the better part of my adult life studying living organisms and the natural forces that shape their forms and habits.

Almost every day I work with aquarium specimens. And almost every day I learn something new and, frankly, fascinating.

Natural aquatic environments owe their uniqueness to a complex interplay of factors. Natural waters may vary widely in composition.

Such physical parameters as temperature, salinity, alkalinity, pH, dissolved gases, and the presence or absence of certain ions all contribute to the specific character of the habitat.

The amount of light available, presence or absence of current, and the type of substrate play an important role.

Thus, a tropical stream is quite unlike a temperate lake, and a coral reef differs sharply from an estuary.

Because each of these environments is different, the types of organisms present varies widely from one environment to another.

Natural environments persist for thousands, or even millions, of years.

Over time, particular types of organisms have adapted to the conditions of the specific environment in which they live.

Fish and invertebrates are distributed in nature according to the habitats for which they are best adapted.

In the aquarium, the same factors that determine the

character of the natural environment can be adjusted to meet the needs of living organisms.

The ideal aquarium is one in which all of the characteristics of a single natural ecosystem are duplicated as closely as possible.

Since nature's diversity is staggering in its scope, each miniature aquatic ecosystem is different, and each is as individual as a work of art.

A marine aquarium represents an investment that should give you and your family pleasure for many years.

Planning for your new tank will help insure that your aquarium inhabitants remain healthy and happy. Here are some basic rules that apply to marine aquariums, which will be repeated and elaborated upon throughout this book:

• Buy the largest aquarium you feel you can accommodate, and outfit it with good quality equipment. This will mean a larger initial expenditure, but will save money in the long run.

• The most important process that takes place in an aquarium is biological filtration, in which ammonia, the primary waste product of fishes and other animals, is converted to nitrate by beneficial bacteria. A thorough understanding of this process is central to your success with any marine aquarium.

• You must familiarize yourself with certain aspects of water chemistry, the physics of lighting and hydraulics, and aspects of the biology of marine life in order to have long term success with a marine aquarium.

• Planning is important. Read books on marine aquariums, observe tanks that others have set up, and those in public aquariums. Discuss your plans with others. In this way, you will maximize your enjoyment, and get the most for your money.

• Your aquarium will require maintenance. Recognize this, and plan to spend at least one hour a week doing routine maintenance on the aquarium. If you make this small time commitment, you will be rewarded with a beautiful, healthy aquarium. Without proper maintenance, problems are an absolute certainty.

• As several other authors have pointed out, perhaps the single most important factor in determining the success or failure of any reef tank is the quality and quantity of the live rock used. Above all, do not scrimp on this important component.

Each of these themes will be discussed more fully elsewhere in this book. Each is discussed by other authors, whose works are listed in the bibliography.

Study this information carefully, and apply your common sense.

And above all, have fun creating your own private piece of the sea's greatest treasure — the living coral reef.

Chapter One

Basic Equipment

If one of your desires is to start a reef tank, this book is designed with your needs in mind. I plan to discuss how to set up a reef system aquarium, using methods that I know will work for you.

We will look at each phase of the process, in order that your progress in getting the tank set up and running will go smoothly. I will cover choosing equipment, and the all-important planning that you should do before you begin.

If you start now, the system should be ready to fill with seawater in a month's time. In a year, you will have a thriving reef tank. Yes, a year. You must have patience. The tank will look great in a few months, but it will look wonderful after a year has passed, if you follow the advice given in this book.

We all have heard the old cliche' "An ounce of prevention is worth a pound of cure." This adage is especially true when it comes to setting up a reef system aquarium.

Planning that you do now will pay off later in lessened maintenance, healthier animals, and fewer headaches.

I will indicate clearly what equipment I regard as essential, and which items I regard as options. In all cases, optional equipment is that which I regard as "essential" for an "ideal" system, but which is not absolutely necessary, especially if you are willing to devote extra effort to regular maintenance.

Put off purchasing optional equipment until later, if your budget requires, and concentrate now on a good quality, basic system. If you are fortunate enough to afford some of the options from the beginning, by all means invest in them.

There is another old saying that goes "If you can't spend money, you must spend time." Most of the optional equipment I will discuss does indeed save maintenance time, by automating routine work that you can do manually.

But such equipment, if of good quality and reliable performance, can cost a lot of money. Only you can weigh the pros and cons of purchasing such equipment. One thing is certain, however. No equipment, no matter how sophisticated and costly, can substitute for your judgment and skill as an aquarist.

Start by choosing the tank. Buy the largest one your space and budget can accommodate. In my opinion, the best tank for most people is one with a base 48 X 18 inches, i.e., a 75 gallon tank. With any reef aquarium system, however, the bigger, the better.

The first decision you will need to make with regard to the system is whether to have the tank drilled, with an internal prefilter, or to use an external prefilter.

Either approach has advantages as well as disadvantages. A prefilter serves two functions. One is to allow for removal of surface water from the tank, and to direct water into the wet/dry filter (trickling filter).

The other function is to trap large particulate matter in a spot from which it can be conveniently and frequently removed and discarded.

External prefilters rely on siphons to remove water from the tank, and must be designed to insure that the siphon will restart in the event of a power failure.

Drilling a glass tank should be done by a professional glass shop, or at the factory that builds the tank.

Installation of a prefilter in a drilled tank must be done in such a way as to insure that the prefilter seams will not leak, allowing the tank to drain.

However, with a drilled tank, there is little likelihood of the flow of water being interrupted after a power outage. In any case, the prefilter should be easily accessible for service, as it should be cleaned about once a week.

After deciding on the prefilter, select a wet/dry filtration system that will hold enough media for the tank you have chosen.

There are many good brands of filters on the market. Choose one that offers quality construction, ample room for filter media, and a price consistent with your budget.

Every brand of wet/dry filter accomplishes biological

filtration in exactly the same way. The differences lie mostly in features that make maintenance convenient and allow easy installation of other equipment.

Below are listed some of the features that I have found to be desirable. Unfortunately, not every brand of wet/dry filter incorporates all of them.

— Built-in protein skimmer, preferably venturi type (see below for more on skimmers)

— Sump compartment same height as biological chamber (this maximizes sump capacity, lessening overflow danger)

— Drip tray (rather than rotating sprayer, which will eventually jam and stop turning)

— Drip tray designed to pull out like a drawer, for easy cleaning

— Slanted plate beneath biological chamber, directs detritus toward sump, from which it is easily removed

— Built-in slots for activated carbon, Poly-Filter™, and other chemical media e.g. Superchem.

— Built-in holder for pH and redox probes (and any other electrodes you may wish to install)

— Threaded PVC fittings through sump for connection of pump and other equipment

— Biological chamber predrilled for air inlets (see below)

— Warranty against leakage (at least one year, preferably longer)

Many of these features can be found in the better lines of wet/dry filters (Ed. note : also referred to as trickle or trickling filters).

In addition, consider the size of the sump portion of the filter. It should be able to hold enough water to prevent an overflow if power is shut off to the tank, and all plumbing is allowed to drain into the filter sump.

Critical to the "engineering" of your reef system is the pump. Buy a good one, with plenty of capacity. A shoddy pump can be relied upon only to fail eventually, and as Thiel and others have pointed out, the pump is the heart of the system.

If it goes out at an inconvenient time (and Murphy's Law virtually guarantees this will be the case) you and your reef are out of luck. For a 75 gallon tank, you will need a pump that will deliver at least 375 gallons per hour AT THE POINT OF DISCHARGE INTO THE TANK.

Most pumps are rated in gallons per hour at one foot of head pressure. "Head pressure" is the distance from the inlet of the pump to the discharge point.

In most reef systems, this will be at least four feet. However, other factors affect working head pressure in a reef tank.

Each 90 degree bend in the return plumbing will add about a foot of "head" because of the friction of the water moving around the bend. Also as a result of friction, each 10 foot horizontal run of pipe will add a foot of head pressure. If part of the pump discharge is shunted to a protein skimmer, this will also rob the tank of flow.

When all of these effects are added up, you will probably

need a pump of about 750 gallons per hour rating for a 75 gallon tank.

Good pumps cost more than poor quality ones, of course. Even if you are on a very tight budget, DO NOT SCRIMP ON THE PUMP.

The plumbing necessary to connect the prefilter to the filter, and to return water from the pump to the tank, must be carefully considered.

No two systems are alike in this respect, and you should make a sketch of your planned plumbing system, giving careful thought to the location of valves, etc., before you purchase the parts you will need.

Two pieces of special equipment for plumbing the filter system should be considered.

There should be a backflow prevention valve located in the return line from the pump to the tank, to prevent back siphoning of water through the pump in the event of a power failure.

Second, a float switch installed in the filter sump, and controlling power to the pump, should be used to prevent the pump running dry should the flow of water from the tank be interrupted. This can happen when a prefilter loses siphon flow, or when the drain from the prefilter becomes clogged.

If you have had little experience with plumbing, it is wise to seek the advice of a friend, plumber or reef system dealer when designing your system.

Select a good quality heater, preferably the submersible type, and install it in the sump of the wet/dry filter. Allow about 3 watts of heating capacity per gallon of water in the system. A 75 gallon system would normally have a 250-watt heater installed, since this is the heater size nearest the required capacity. It would be better to use two 150-watt heaters for this set-up, rather than one 250-watt.

That way, if one heater fails, there will still be some heating capacity. The likelihood of both heaters failing simultaneously is small.

There is no benefit in purchasing a heater larger than the required capacity for the system. If a 100 watt heater will raise the temperature of the tank 5 degrees in two hours, a 200-watt heater will raise the temperature of the same tank 5 degrees in one hour.

In other words, a larger heater will simply raise the temperature of the water faster.

Rapid changes in water conditions are to be avoided in reef tanks.

In addition to the wet/dry filter system, its pump and associated plumbing, and the heater, three pieces of equipment are often included in reef set-ups.

These are protein skimmer, ozonizer, and redox controller. I consider a protein skimmer to be necessary, and the other two to be optional equipment.

Two types of protein skimmer are available: columnar and venturi. The one I like best is the venturi type. Although any protein skimmer will remove organic matter from the tank, for maximum efficiency, choose the correct size.

Venturi skimmers require a canister filter or other pump to circulate water from the tank through the skimmer.

Some types of columnar skimmers require a separate pump, as well. In fact, there is a bewildering array of skimmer designs and sizes.

There are wet/dry filters available with the protein skimmer already built in.

You will need a good, high volume air pump to provide air to the protein skimmer, if it is a columnar type. Good air pumps are available at any aquarium shop. Choose one that is larger than you think you will need; it is hard to have too much air available.

Similarly, if you are unsure about the choice of skimmer, choose a larger one. Most reef-keeping experts agree that it is not possible to over-skim the aquarium.

For more information on the pros and cons of protein skimmers, consult Albert J. Thiel's excellent book "*The Marine Fish and Invert Reef Aquarium*"(Aardvark Press), or Martin Moe's "*The Marine Aquarium Reference: Systems and Invertebrates*"(Green Turtle Press).

Both of these books should be in your library if you are planning a reef tank.

The advantages and disadvantages of different types of protein skimmers can be summarized as follows.

Columnar skimmers that are designed to go inside the tank itself are simple, foolproof, and relatively inexpensive. They are, however, bulky and their presence in the tank detracts from the overall natural appearance.

External columnar skimmers are more expensive, because they must be made leakproof.

In addition, such a skimmer, especially for a large tank,

must have a tall column to maximize the contact time between the air bubbles and the water.

Thus, the skimmer may not fit under the aquarium cabinet, out of sight. All columnar skimmers rely on airstones to create a stream of very fine bubbles.

These will need periodic replacement. Further, as the airstones begin to clog with use, the air supply will require periodic adjustment, in order to keep the skimmer operating properly. Venturi skimmers, on the other hand, do not employ airstones, but rather use a venturi valve to produce a mix of water and fine bubbles.

Therefore, there are no airstones to replace, and adjustments do not have to be made frequently to keep the skimmer working.

Venturi skimmers are also designed to create a spinning vortex of water and air inside the skimmer, to maximize contact time between the air and water, without the necessity of a tall column.

Thus, a venturi skimmer for a given size aquarium will always be smaller than a comparable columnar skimmer (foam fractionator).

The small size means that the venturi skimmer can easily be hidden underneath the tank, and will leave more room in the cabinet for other equipment.

The primary drawback to venturi skimmers is their relatively greater cost than comparable columnar types.

A protein skimmer can also be used as the reaction chamber for ozone, if you choose to add an ozonizer to your system.

Ozone is a highly reactive form of oxygen gas. It is usually produced by an electrical discharge device, and has a peculiar odor.

In the aquarium, ozone is used to oxidize complex organic molecules, making them available for degradation by heterotrophic bacteria.

Use of ozone in the reef tank will help to keep the oxidation-reduction potential of the aquarium at a desirable level, about 350-400 millivolts. If you decide to add an ozonizer to your system, you should also install a redox potential controller.

Redox potential controllers are electronic devices that measure the oxidation-reduction potential of the aquarium, and control the operation of the ozonizer to maintain the tank at a preset millivolt reading, in much the same way that a thermostat regulates the temperature of your house by controlling the heating system.

These units are expensive, usually around $500, but are essential for adequate control of the rate at which ozone is introduced into the tank.

Adding too little ozone has no harmful effect, although this would be a very inefficient use of the ozonizer and no marked results would ensue.

Too much ozone, however, can be detrimental to the health of the tank's inhabitants. Since every tank is different in terms of the amount of ozone that will be required to maintain an oxidation-reduction potential of 350-400 mV, an automatic controller is, in my opinion, the only way to go.

Remember that an ozone system is a desirable, but not necessary, component of a reef tank.

Get your aquarium set up and running, and add an ozone system later on, if you desire.

If you do decide on using ozone, buy the ozonizer and redox controller at the same time, and follow the manufacturer's instructions for installation.

You can expect to spend about $700 for the whole system, not counting an air pump to supply air to the ozonizer. This can be the same pump that you were using for the protein skimmer, and the skimmer itself, as I mentioned above, can be used as the reaction chamber for introducing ozone.

One final note about ozone. Many plastics will be degraded by ozone gas. You should use only materials that are known to be ozone resistant for making connections between the ozonizer and the reaction chamber.

Also, use an ozone-resistant check valve between the ozonizer and the reaction chamber, to prevent water from siphoning into the ozonizer should a power failure occur.

Seawater and ozone discharge electrodes do not mix! Serious damage, and a potential electrical hazard, can occur if water reaches the electrode during a power outage, and power is then subsequently restored.

You can also locate the ozonizer above the water level, to prevent siphoning from occurring.

For more information about oxidation reduction potential and redox controllers, see Chapter Six.

Ultraviolet (UV) sterilizers perform some of the same functions as ozonizers. The primary function of a UV sterilizer, however, is to destroy harmful microorganisms that may be present in the water, as an aid to disease prevention in the aquarium.

While use of UV will not prevent a disease outbreak from occurring, it will help to minimize the risk of disease developing in your fishes.

In order to work effectively, a UV sterilizer will require periodic cleaning, as slime and bacteria will build up inside the unit, reducing the penetration of UV light into the water flowing through the sterilizer.

Also, you will need to replace the UV lamp in the unit about every six months, in order to maintain its effectiveness.

If I were choosing between an ozone system and UV, I would select ozone first, and maybe add the UV later, and only if the tank were heavily stocked with fish. Since reef tanks typically do not have a heavy fish population, UV sterilization is of limited benefit.

Finally, let's consider the options with regard to lighting the tank. Bear in mind that the lighting system is at least as important as the filtration system, if not more so.

Over a typical four foot tank, such as a 75 gallon, you will need four 40-watt fluorescent lamps, or a metal halide system. For tanks over four feet long, or for a very deep tank (depth greater than 20 inches), metal halide is more satisfactory. We will have more to say about lighting systems in Chapter Three.

For now, here follows a brief discussion of what has worked for me.

If you are using fluorescent lighting, you will need a fixture that can accommodate four 40-watt lamps.

Of these, two should be Actinic 03 lamps (TL40W03). The other two can be either daylight (F40D) or 5000K Ultralume lamps (F40/50U), or one of each.

Using daylight lamps will impart a more bluish appearance to the tank, while using the Ultralumes will impart a more "natural" appearance.

Either one is satisfactory for the majority of species of invertebrates with which I have had experience (several hundred kinds).

Macroalgae seem to prefer the daylight lamps, and these should be used if you plan to include macroalgae in your reef tank.

If you opt for metal halide lighting, a fixture holding two 175-watt lamps is sufficient for a six-foot tank (e.g., a 135 gallon), or for a very deep tank (e.g., a 110 gallon "show" tank).

Use either the new 5500K lamps now available, or use a fixture that includes Actinic 03 fluorescent lamps.

Both types are available from Energy Savers Unlimited. Consult their advertisements for more information.

I have been asked repeatedly about my opinion of the various types of new lamps that are now available for fluorescent lighting systems, and about the relative merits of various brands of lamps. In my opinion, there are many combinations and many brands of lamps that give entirely satisfactory results.

The ones I have recommended above have proven themselves in my tanks, and I see no reason to change, especially if there is a significant increased cost involved in doing so. In the case of metal halide lamps, and their alleged potentially detrimental effects on certain types of invertebrates, I have seen no evidence to support this contention. What is needed is a series of controlled, long-term experiments evaluating the various types of lighting systems.

Too many times "evidence" is produced to support one hypothesis or another, in complete absence of what scientists call a "control".

A typical scenario runs something like this: A tank is set up with one lighting system and the animals do not appear to be doing well. So a new lighting system is installed. Now the animals appear better. Conclusion: the new lighting system is better.

This is nonsense. What one really needs in order to evaluate the relative merits of the two lighting systems is two tanks, one with each of the two types of lighting.

With the exception of the lighting differences, these two tanks must be as nearly identical in all respects as can possibly be achieved. After several months of evaluation and comparison of the health, growth, etc. of the inhabitants in each tank, one can perhaps conclude that one type of lighting is "better" than another.

Otherwise, one cannot say for certain whether the lighting is responsible for the observed results, or whether other factors are involved. The practice of drawing "scientific" conclusions based upon "experiments" carried out without appropriate controls is commonplace in the aquarium hobby, and should be discouraged.

More information about lighting systems appears in Chapter Three.

This concludes our discussion of the major equipment you will need for a reef tank.

To summarize, you will need, at minimum, the tank itself, an internal or external prefilter, a wet/dry filter, a water pump, miscellaneous plumbing connections, a heater, and a lighting system.

You should also install a protein skimmer, which means you will need another water pump or a canister filter to operate the skimmer, and an air pump if you select a columnar skimmer.

Air should also be directed into the biological chamber of the wet/dry filter, and this may require a second air pump, although a large pump can supply both needs.

Optional equipment would consist of an ozonizer and redox potential controller, along with appropriate ozone-resistant tubing and a check valve.

It is also a good idea to install a powerhead or two in the tank itself, to create additional water movement. There are even devices available that will allow automatic switching between two powerheads to produce a pulsed flow simulating tidal currents. This is a good, but idea.

Purchase a thermometer to measure the temperature of the tank, which should be about 75 degrees Fahrenheit.

You may also find it desirable to have a timer or timers to switch the lights on an off on a regular schedule.

All this equipment requires electricity, of course. Plan on having a sufficient number of electrical outlets near the tank, to accommodate all of the power cords that you will be using.

For safety's sake, use special ground fault interrupt outlets that are designed for safe operation in wet areas.

Consult your electrician for information if you are in doubt as to the safety or adequacy of the electrical supply to the aquarium.

Spend some time planning your set-up, shopping for the equipment you will need, assembling the system, and getting things up and running. I recommend testing the finished system with freshwater before adding the salt mix and starting the cycling process.

This will insure that everything is working properly, and that there are no leaks in the plumbing, etc.

Also, flushing the system with freshwater will remove dust, dirt, and plastic solvents that may be present. Should a problem develop at this stage, you will not have wasted gallons of expensive salt mix.

And, lastly, select a good quality salt mix for making up the synthetic seawater for the tank. Many good mixes are widely available. We will have more to say about salt mixes in the next chapter.

In conclusion, we have briefly covered the equipment required for a reef system aquarium. I urge you to consult your dealer, various books, and magazine articles to help you decide on exactly what brands of equipment you should purchase.

The brand names mentioned in this book are those with which I have had personal experience, and are not the only ones on the market.

Finally, remember that equipment selection is only half the process of establishing a reef tank.

Even with the best equipment, you will have problems if you do not understand the importance of water quality, biological and other types of filtration, and the biological needs of the animals you will be keeping.

We will cover these topics in the chapters that follow.

For now, read, plan, shop around, get the tank set up and the equipment installed and tested.

Chapter Two

Seawater and Biological Filtration

In Chapter One, we covered the equipment needed for setting up a reef tank. Let's briefly review.

Start by choosing the size tank you are going to set up. Select a wet/dry filter system that is appropriate for the tank you choose.

This basically means that the filter should be able to hold enough biological filter medium to support the life forms you will be keeping.

Choose a pump that will turn over the entire volume of the system about 3 - 5 times per hour.

Optional, but recommended, accessories for the filter system include a float switch to shut off the pump in case water flow to the filter is interrupted, and a check valve between the pump and the tank, to prevent back siphoning of water in the event of a power failure.

I highly recommend adding a protein skimmer. Optional

equipment would include an ozone generator and redox potential controller.

Every reef tank needs a reliable heater, an accurate thermometer, and a powerhead or two to create water movement.

Pay particular attention to lighting installed on your reef system.

No filtration system, regardless of its level of sophistication, will allow you to keep corals, anemones, and similar invertebrates without adequate lighting.

Once you have chosen and installed the equipment, and have run the system with freshwater for a day or two to check for leaks and to flush out dirt and solvents, it is time to fill the tank with synthetic seawater.

As Thiel and other authors have pointed out, to the inhabitants of your tank, the water in it is like the air is to us.

Fish and invertebrates "breathe" water, and ingest it constantly.

Invertebrates such as corals and anemones are largely composed of seawater, and the proportions of chemicals in their body fluids largely reflect the proportions found in the water around them.

Thus, it is absolutely vital to insure that the water in the reef tank is of good quality.

When mention is made of water quality, hobbyists generally think about the ability of the filtration system to maintain good conditions in the tank.

But water quality actually begins with the freshwater and salt mix used to prepare synthetic seawater for the aquarium.

Let's consider each of these in turn.

The reef keeper has two alternatives with regard to the basic water supply. Either use straight tap water, or purify tap water in some way to render it more suitable for aquarium use.

As I gain more experience with reef keeping, I have found that using straight tap water is usually quite unsatisfactory.

Municipal water supplies often contain high levels of contaminants, that, while regarded as safe for human consumption, are not suitable for delicate marine life.

Such contaminants include phosphate, nitrate, copper, lead, aluminum, other heavy metals, mud, and organic matter, not to mention chlorine and chloramine.

Ideally, aquarists would use only glass-distilled water for making up seawater. This type of water is used in research labs, and for delicate aquaculture work. Unfortunately, glass distilled water is expensive to prepare.

For example, a still that will produce 12 gallons of glass-distilled water per day costs $1195.00 (plus shipping, installation, pretreatment cartridges, and special holding tank), according to the catalog listing of a major scientific supply house.

Steam distilled water, usually available at grocery stores, costs about a dollar a gallon, and usually contains traces of copper from the still. Thus, it is unsatisfactory for aquarium use.

The hobbyist is left therefore with two practical methods of preparing water for mixing seawater.

One method, which has proven best for me, is the use of a reverse osmosis unit to purify tap water. Such units are only moderately expensive (around $200), easy to install, and can produce enough water to meet the needs of the average tank for only a few pennies per day.

Reverse osmosis systems work by using water pressure from the supply line to force water through a special membrane that filters out most of the pollutants, producing a purified product water that is suitable for reef aquarium use.

If you cannot afford a reverse osmosis system, you can greatly improve the quality of your tap water by using some standard aquarium filtration equipment to "prefilter" your synthetic seawater before it is added to your tank. Here is how to do this.

• Set up a container that will hold enough water to meet your needs.

This can be anything from a spare aquarium tank to a plastic trash can. Depending upon the quantity of water you plan to prepare, purchase a standard aquarium power filter.

I use the Marineland Magnum 330 filter, because it can be used with both carbon and diatomaceous earth cartridges.

Also purchase a supply of good quality marine grade activated carbon, some diatomaceous earth powder, and a supply of Poly-Filter™.

Fill your container with the required amount of tap

water, and set up the power filter with diatomaceous earth only. Filter the tap water for 12 to 24 hours to remove mud and suspended solids.

Now change out the filter cartridge, and replace with activated carbon and Poly-Filter™. (If you use the Magnum carbon container, you can wrap the Poly-Filter™ around the container, and secure it with rubber bands.) Filter the tap water for another 24 hours, then add your salt mix.

Continue filtration to aid in dissolving the salt mix, and adjust the specific gravity to match that of your tank. If you carry out this procedure, you will have a very good quality synthetic seawater ready to add to the tank.

Use a pH test kit to check the pH of the newly made water, making sure the kit is for saltwater use.

It is ready to use when the pH stabilizes at 8.2. If you locate your mixing container in the garage or other area where the temperature is apt to be lower than that of the tank, purchase an aquarium heater to keep the temperature of the mixing container at 75 degrees.

Both the carbon and the Poly-Filter™ can be re-used for several batches of water. Seal them in a plastic bag and store in the refrigerator, after rinsing with chlorinated tap water to help prevent bacterial growth. Discard both when the color change of the Poly-Filter™ indicates that it is no longer functional.

If all this seems like too much trouble, go ahead and buy the reverse osmosis unit. Your reef tank will be better for it.

Now that you have the means to produce purified water to start with, give careful consideration to the quality of the salt mix you use. There are many brands of synthetic seawater mix available.

The cheapest mix may not be a good buy in the long run, because both purity and formulation can vary. On the other hand, there are expensive mixes that are just that, expensive, but not necessarily better.

In my opinion, the best way to select a salt mix is to prepare a small batch, using purified water made as I described above, and then run a few tests when the water is ready to use.

Check pH first, it should be 8.2-8.3. Next check alkalinity. It should be in the range of 3.5 to 5.0 milliequivalents per liter. Tests for both nitrate and phosphate should be below the range of most test kits, i.e., less than 0.1 ppm for phosphate, and less than 10 ppm for nitrate.

If you don't have these test kits, buy them before you continue with your reef system set-up. When you have located a brand of salt that meets these criteria, stick with it.

For filling the tank initially, you can use the tank itself as the mixing container. If you do not use a reverse osmosis system, filter the tank in the manner I described above. Do not use the tank's filtration system for this purpose, since all this will accomplish is trapping within the system all the pollutants you are trying to eliminate.

To summarize:

1) flush the display tank first with freshwater to check for leaks and wash out dirt and contaminants,

2) drain the tank, and refill with filtered synthetic seawater.

Now you are ready to start the filtration system, and begin the process of "cycling" the biological filter.

For this procedure, you need not run either the protein skimmer or ozone, and you should not have Poly-Filter™ in the system.

Carbon is OK, but Poly-Filter™ removes ammonia, nitrite and nitrates, and its presence may retard the progress of the cycling process. Add Poly-Filter™ later, after the tank is cycled and animals are added.

When looking at chemical filtering media, check out SuperChem as well. This, too, is an excellent product.

Many varied recommendations have been made as to the best way to get a biological filter going properly. Some authors advocate using hardy, inexpensive fish, such as black mollies or damsels, as the initial source of ammonia.

Others recommend live rock. And still others, including myself, advocate adding ammonia in chemical form, e.g. Goldstart or similar products.

Each method works, and each method involves two primary components: a source of ammonia, and a starter culture of nitrifying bacteria.

First, let's consider the ammonia source. If you use fish or live rock, ammonia enters the system as a result of the natural metabolism of living organisms. Some authors regard this as a "better" form of ammonia. I know of no evidence to support this contention.

Nitrifying bacteria are grown under laboratory conditions with only inorganic ammonia sources, such as ammonium chloride, and there is ample evidence that they grow happily under aquarium conditions on this ammonia source, as well.

If you feel that using an organic ammonia source is better, by all means do so, as the end result will be the same.

I prefer to start with inorganic ammonium chloride, as a 6% solution in water. Add enough to produce a test reading of 3.0 ppm. This will take about 1.5 ml of ammonium chloride solution per eight gallons of tank water.

Check the ammonia reading after 24 hours. It may be lower than the original reading, owing to the formation of amines as the ammonia reacts with other compounds present, and as a result of "outgassing" of ammonia gas due to aeration.

Add more ammonium chloride to bring the reading back to 3 ppm, and check and readjust again after 24 hours. Once the ammonia level stabilizes at around 3 ppm after a 24 hour wait, you are ready to add a starter culture of nitrifying bacteria to the tank.

There are now on the market a variety of products that purport to contain live nitrifying bacteria in a "pre-served" state for use in starting a biological filter.

In my experience these products are ineffective.

For many years, I worked in a microbiological research laboratory, and gained experience with many types of bacteria, including *Nitrosomonas* and *Nitrobacter*, the principal genera of nitrifiers present in aquariums.

These nitrifying bacteria are extremely difficult to pre-serve alive for any period of time, even when using sophisticated methods such as freezing them in liquid nitrogen.

Because of the difficulty of preservation, our laboratory would routinely order live cultures of these organisms directly from the American Type Culture Collection.

The ATCC is a repository for thousands of species of bacteria and other organisms that are used in everything from biomedical research to industrial processes, and their reputation for expertise in the culture of microorganisms is unparalleled.

Even with starter cultures of nitrifiers from the ATCC, about 50% of the time we were unable to produce active cultures. Quite simply, these bacteria are very difficult to maintain in culture, and nearly impossible to preserve in a living state. Therefore, the likelihood of getting a viable culture from an off-the-shelf product made for aquarium hobbyist use is almost zero.

Fortunately, there is an alternative. All you need is a handful of sand, gravel, or other substrate material from an existing aquarium that has a healthy, active biological filter bed.

Many dealers are happy to provide this material, and some even set up special tanks just for maintaining a supply of live nitrifying bacteria. You may also have a hobbyist friend who will part with a small amount of "starter gravel."

Do not be concerned about the possibility of introducing parasites or other undesirable organisms along with the bacteria, since the whole cycling process will take about a month, and it is highly unlikely that such undesirable organisms will survive in your tank for that period of time.

Of course, it would be unwise to accept material from a tank containing diseased fish or invertebrates, for two reasons:

1) medications that may have been used in the tank may be present in the starter material, and

2) chances are the filter in the source tank may be in bad shape to begin with, as otherwise the fish would be in better health.

Live rock is also an excellent source of beneficial bacteria, as every cranny and crevice of the rock is usually heavily colonized with these organisms. Using live rock has other benefits, as we shall see in Chapter Four.

For now, suffice it to say that you can introduce live rock as a source for nitrifying bacteria. You can add one small piece, or several pounds. The more you add, the faster the cycling process will go to completion.

In any case, after you have added ammonia and a source of live bacteria to the system, wait about five days, and begin testing for both ammonia and nitrite. Test every few days, and keep a record of your results.

You should see the level of ammonia begin to decrease, and this will be accompanied by a rise in the level of nitrites. That is because *Nitrosomonas* is busy converting the ammonia to nitrite.

Ammonia is inhibitory to *Nitrobacter*, and this organism remains in a dormant state for a while until the ammonia level drops sufficiently for it to begin growing. *Nitrobacter* uses nitrite as its food, converting this compound into nitrate.

You will find that nitrite levels tend to rise very high

during the cycling process, but once the *Nitrobacter* "kicks in" nitrites will begin to decline, and consequently nitrate levels will increase.

You can check this with a nitrate test kit, if you wish. Once all of the nitrite has been converted into nitrate, the nitrite reading will be zero, and the cycling process is complete.

At this point, which is usually about a month after the whole process was initiated, you are almost ready to begin stocking the tank. All that remains is to change 100% of the water in the system. Why? Because the end product of the cycling process, nitrate, will still be present.

Nitrate is harmful to many species of invertebrates. Some tangs will refuse to eat when nitrate concentrations are high. Undesirable algae growth will be encouraged by the presence of nitrates.

Since your goal is to provide the highest possible water quality for the animals that you will be adding over the next few months, why not start with clean, freshly prepared seawater mix?

Make sure that both temperature and specific gravity of the new water are identical to the old water, lest you slow down the metabolism of the beneficial bacteria you have spent the last few weeks culturing.

Finally, remember that the waste product of living animals (ammonia) is "food" to the biological filter bacteria, and that all the food that you originally added as ammonium chloride solution is now used up.

Therefore, add a few animals to the tank as soon as possible after the cycle is complete.

Since this is a reef tank, you will probably add live rock as the next step.

However, live rock does not produce much ammonia, and neither do many of the other invertebrates that you will be keeping.

Thus, the level of beneficial bacteria in the filter system may decline somewhat, owing to the absence of food to sustain their growth.

If you plan to keep fish in your reef tank, it is wise to go ahead and add a couple of specimens along with the live rock, in order to keep the biological filter fully functional.

Chapter Three

Light and Lighting Systems

Apart from water conditions, the single most important factor in the success of a reef tank is the quantity and quality of the light provided.

So much has been written about lighting systems and their pros and cons that the average hobbyist is often confused as to the best choices for lighting.

Before we go into the details of choosing a lighting system, here are a few points about lighting that you should keep in mind.

You need a lighting system that provides, ideally, 10,000 lumens or more of light per square meter of aquarium surface being illuminated.

You cannot compensate for a lack of light intensity, either by increasing the period of time that the lights are on, or by using wide spectrum lamps.

However, assuming the intensity of the light is sufficient, you should use lamps that have a high Kelvin degree rating, above 5000, if possible.

Yours truly was perhaps the first American author to point out this fact in a hobbyist magazine, in an article that appeared in the April, 1982 issue of *Freshwater and Marine Aquarium* magazine.

Little notice was taken of this significant revelation until the publication of George Smit's landmark series of articles several years later, in which he introduced the concept of wet/dry filtration to American aquarists.

This new filtration concept grabbed the hobbyists' attention so firmly that the equally important concept of lighting was relegated to second place.

Even today, the topic of reef tank lighting is fraught with more confusion, misunderstanding, and false claims than any other aspect of reef aquarium keeping, despite all that has been written on the subject by authors such as Burleson, Delbeek, Hoff, Moe, Smit, Spotte, Sprung, Thiel and others.

I will attempt to sort out some of this confusion, in order to permit readers to make an informed decision about the type of lighting that should be used for a reef tank set-up.

Photobiologists, scientists who study the interactions between living organisms and light, measure light intensity in terms of "photon irradiance".

Simply put, this is a measure of the number of "photons" (light energy units) falling on a given area — of coral reef or cornfield — at a given moment.

Why use such a measurement? Because energy is what

drives living systems. For photosynthetic organisms the amount of light energy reaching them determines how well the vital engine of photosynthesis runs.

You can think of this situation as being similar to the relationship between the accelerator pedal (light intensity) and the speed of your car's engine (photosynthesis).

Press down on the pedal (increase the light intensity) and the engine revs up (rate of photosynthesis increases).

Just as your car runs best at moderate, as opposed to very slow or very high, speeds, so also is there an optimum level of "acceleration " for photosynthesis.

Photobiologists have learned that the total number of photons (intensity) falling on a given organism is more important than the energy level (wavelength) of individual photons.

How then, is the aquarist going to insure that this energy requirement is met? Unless you have access to the necessary (and expensive) instrumentation to measure photon irradiance underwater, your best bet is to rely upon the old-style method of measuring light intensity in lumens and irradiance in lux (lumens per square meter).

Over tropical seas, irradiance can exceed 150,000 lux, far more intense than any aquarist can hope to achieve over a tank. Fortunately, 10,000 lux is sufficient for most reef organisms, although more than this is certainly not harmful.

Thus, to determine the light intensity required for a reef tank, first calculate the surface area of the tank in square meters. One square foot equals .093 square meters. So the surface area of a 55 gallon tank (about 4 square feet) is about .37 square meters.

Multiplying this value by the number given above, 10,000 lumens per square meter, yields 3700 lumens for the minimum amount of light that must reach the organisms in the tank.

How can one determine which lamps will provide this much light? That's the easy part, because lighting manufacturers provide this data in the specification sheets they publish for every type of lamp they make.

For example, according to the Phillips Lighting catalog, one of their 40-watt "Ultralume" fluorescent lamps (F40T12/50U) has an initial lumen output of 3300 lumens. Wow! Drop a couple of these over a 55 gallon tank and there should be plenty of light! Right?

Well, sorry, but some practical matters get in the way. For one thing, all lamps decrease in intensity with use. Thus, we must look at the average lumen output over the life of the lamp. This varies with different lamp types, but is usually somewhere around 60% of the initial output.

That would be 1980 lumens for the "Ultralume" lamp in this example. Two lamps would therefore have an average output of 3960 lumens, enough, according to our earlier calculations.

Wrong again. Our line of reasoning up to this point assumes that all of the light emitted from the lamps will reach the bottom of the tank, and, alas, the laws of physics are against us on this point.

In the first place, in order for the total output of the lamps to reach the surface of the tank, we would need a perfect, 100% efficient, reflector, and, of course, none such exists.

Estimates of reflector efficiency, coupled with allowances for reflection from the water surface, and other factors, reveal that about the best we can hope for is that roughly 50% of the light emitted from the lamps will reach the tank.

That means we will need four of the 40-watt "Ultralumes" in this example to provide a total of 3960 lumens at the water surface. So far, so good, but now we come upon another one of Mother Nature's laws that is working against us.

This is the Inverse Square Law that states, "the intensity of light falling upon a surface decreases in proportion to the square of the distance between the surface and the light source."

For our purposes, this can be translated as "double the distance between the lamps and the bottom of the tank, and you need four times as many lamps."

A 55 gallon tank is about 20 inches deep, and the lamps of necessity will be suspended several inches above the water. Call the total distance between the lamps and the bottom of the tank two feet, and you can see that you will need 16 "Ultralumes" to provide 10,000 lux on the tank bottom!

Let's get practical here. We have all seen reef tanks that do OK with only four 40-watt lamps over the top.

So what gives?

This merely demonstrates, in my opinion, that :

1) our assumptions concerning average lamp output, reflector efficiency, etc., are overly conservative, and

2) marine organisms are marvelously adaptable creatures that can obviously "get by" with less than the optimum amount of light.

After all, it is not always sunny in the tropics, the water is not always crystal clear, and it is not always necessary for *zooxanthellae* to be photosynthesizing at their maximum rate.

All well and good, but did I hear anyone say that they wanted a reef tank in which the corals and other organisms would merely "get by"?

Or would you prefer a tank in which the organisms flourish, grow, and reproduce? The former situation is, in my opinion, improper, if not cruel, tantamount to keeping a puppy or kitten on starvation rations that inhibit growth and lead to disease and early death.

Aquarists far prefer the second situation, where the organisms are vibrant, just as they are on a natural reef. This is the primary reason why I prefer, indeed advocate, the use of metal halide lighting for reef tanks.

A single, 175-watt metal halide lamp generates about 15,000 lumens, and is smaller than a football. I know of no other practical light source for the aquarium that will provide this intensity in so small a space.

What about those stories we have read or heard about metal halide lamps "burning" corals and invertebrates? This is, in my opinion, hogwash.

None of the American made lamps produces enough ultraviolet light to directly cause burning, although certain Osram lamps do need a UV shield, the so-called Power Stars.

The "burning" problem has never happened to me, and I have placed literally hundreds of corals and other polyps beneath metal halide light sources.

Second, even metal halides are not as bright as the sunlight that falls upon these animals in nature.

So where do these "burning" tales come from? I suspect there are three sources for this confusion:

1. To most people, it seems, a "coral" is anything given that name by the dealer from which it was purchased. Many species that are called "corals" are not, but rather are *gorgonians*, *alcyonarians* ("soft corals"), *corallimorphs* ("mushroom corals") or some other type of polyp.

Some of these, certain *gorgonians* and *alcyonarians* especially, come from areas where light intensity is naturally low.

Placing such animals under intense lighting could well have detrimental effects. Try growing a fern in full sun in your yard and you will see by analogy what I mean.

2. Many suppliers do not provide proper lighting for specimens of corals, etc., kept in their holding tanks. If business is slow, and this inventory does not "move" well, the polyps will shed their *zooxanthellae*, taking on a "bleached" appearance.

When such specimens are subsequently placed under bright light, the remaining *zooxanthellae* begin to photosynthesize at a high rate, and to multiply rapidly.

This results in a high rate of oxygen production. Now,

while oxygen is essential for all forms of life, too much is harmful.

Charles Delbeek has pointed out that the detrimental effects of placing a "bleached" specimen under high intensity lighting may be due to oxygen poisoning.

3. Another matter that happens when corals and other polyps are held under conditions of inadequate light, or with specimens that happen to have been collected from shaded waters, is changes in the pigmentation of the *zooxanthellae*.

As we said earlier, *zooxanthellae* are marvelously adaptable. They produce, in addition to chlorophyll, a host of other pigments.

Some of the "accessory" pigments permit the utilization of light wavelengths that chlorophyll does not absorb, enabling the zooxanthellae to capture more of the sun's energy, and to take advantage of as much as possible of the light spectra available at different depths, on cloudy days, etc.

Other pigments are produced in response to ultraviolet light, and serve to shield the *zooxanthellae* and host polyp from the harmful effects of this radiation.

Two things can therefore happen when organisms harboring *zooxanthellae* are shifted from one lighting regime to another.

The proportion of the different accessory pigments may shift, as the *zooxanthellae* accommodate themselves to the new light situation. This may be evident as a color change in the coral, and be interpreted as "burning" by aquarists unaware of the phenomenon.

Alternatively, organisms from deeper waters, or specimens that have languished for too long in dim light, may have ceased production of those pigments that shield them from ultraviolet radiation.

When these are subsequently placed under bright lights, the effect is similar to that experienced by someone who, having spent a long winter indoors, rushes out on the first sunny day, stripped to his swimming trunks, and spends an afternoon sunbathing. Ouch! Get the Solarcaine! (Thanks again to Charles Delbeek for this apt analogy.)

As you can see, the alleged "burning" of corals by metal halide lights can, in almost every case, be attributed to a lack of understanding of how these organisms respond to light, and not to any inherent detrimental effect of the lights themselves.

In summary, the best all around lighting source for your reef aquarium is metal halide. This is the most practical way to achieve the high light intensity necessary for photosynthesis by the *zooxanthellae*.

Fluorescent lighting can certainly be used, but care must be taken to insure that enough lamps are provided to give sufficient intensity.

What about the quality of the light, its spectral characteristics, or, if you prefer, its "color"? Natural sunlight, the ideal light source for the reef aquarium (albeit an impractical one), is composed of many wavelengths ("colors") of light.

We want a light source that duplicates the spectrum of sunlight as closely as possible. One reason for this is that photosynthetic organisms produce pigments that enable them to utilize a variety of wavelengths.

This maximizes the amount of energy they can capture from the light they receive, and allows them to carry out photosynthesis under varying conditions of cloudiness, and clarity, and at different times of the day (when the changing angle of the sun results in changes in the wavelengths that actually reach the water).

Fortunately, there is a relatively simple way to compare the spectral output of various light sources to that of natural sunlight.

This is called the "Kelvin temperature" scale.

Without going into the details of how this number is derived, suffice it to say that noonday sun under clear skies has a rating of 5500 degrees Kelvin, or 5500K. This is a bluish white light.

Lower Kelvin temperature ratings will be progressively more red in color, while higher temperatures are progressively more blue.

Thus, the nearer the Kelvin temperature of an artificial lighting source is to 5500K, the more closely this source mimics the spectral quality of natural sunlight.

You can obtain Kelvin temperature data on virtually any lamp by checking the specification sheet for that lamp type, available from the lamp's manufacturer.

The Phillips "Ultralume" fluorescent lamp, used in examples earlier, has a rating of 5000K, very close to sunlight.

Other fluorescent lamps are available with 5500K ratings, and it is possible to combine several types of fluorescent lamps to achieve both high intensity and a suitable spectral rating.

High output (HO) and very high output (VHO) fluorescent lamps are very bright, but remember that these
lamps require special ballasts, and will need to be
changed more frequently than standard fluorescent
lamps, owing to shifts in the spectral output of the lamps
during prolonged use.

Ultralume, Daylight, Vita-Light, Actinic 03, Actinic Day,
Triton, Advantage X, Chroma 50, Chroma 75, the list of
available lamp types is seemingly endless.

Only by experimentation can you determine if a particular combination is going to be satisfactory for your reef
tank, taking into account not only the needs of the
organisms, but also the need for "eye appeal".

Different types of lamps will give different color effects.
One combination that has worked for me is a 1:1 ratio of
Ultralume to Actinic 03, at 3 watts per gallon.

Macroalgae seem to grow better under illumination that
is higher than 5500K. I have achieved good results with
6500K daylight lamps (F40T12D), using two 40-watt
lamps to illuminate a 40 gallon tank (48" X 12" X 16") for
macroalgae, including *Caulerpa* (several species),
Penicillus, *Halimeda*, *Udotea*, *Cymopolia*, *Valonia*,
Dictyosphaerium, *Gracillaria*, *Hypnea*, and several others.

All of these species, as well as corals and anemones, do
well under metal halide lighting, however.

Unless you are color blind, you can make a good guess
about the Kelvin degree rating of an unknown lamp by
comparing the appearance of an object illuminated by
this lamp with the appearance of the same object under
natural daylight on a clear day.

Another approach is to photograph the same object in daylight and under the lamp in question, using a film designed for daylight photography, and compare the appearance of the prints.

These techniques will also work when experimenting with different combinations of lamps, since you cannot simply "combine" the Kelvin temperature ratings in some way to determine the overall rating for the combination, even if you have this information for each of the lamps individually.

In metal halide lamps, Energy Savers Unlimited makes available 100 and 175-watt lamp with a 5500K rating. These are, in my opinion, the best available light source for any reef aquarium.

Other metal halide lamps impart a yellowish coloration to the organisms in the tank, which is not harmful, but is not pleasing to the eye, either.

This can be corrected by adding one 40-watt Actinic 03 lamp (TL40W03) for each 175 watt metal halide lamp used.

Assuming that you opt for the best, and use 5500K metal halide lighting for your reef tank, pay attention to the following important safeguards.

Never look directly at the filament of the lamp; all metal halides produce at least some UV, which can damage your eyes, and in any case the lamps are dazzlingly bright.

Locate the ballast in an area where it will be well-ventilated — all lamp ballasts produce heat — and protect the ballast (and all other electrical equipment around the aquarium) from contact with seawater.

If there is a spill DISCONNECT THE POWER immediately before cleaning up.

Finally, suspend metal halide lamps above the water, to avoid radiant heating, and to provide ample room to work on the tank without bumping into the light fixtures.

And of course, make sure the fixtures are securely mounted. You do not want a hot glass object operated at high voltage to fall into the tank!

Operate the lighting system for 12 hours per day, to mimic the day/night cycle in the tropics. Using a timer to create a consistent cycle is a good idea.

Incidentally, it makes no difference to the fish and invertebrates if the lights come on at 8:00 A.M., noon, or 10:00 P.M., as long as a consistent routine is maintained.

Set the timer to turn the lights on and off according to the dictates of your personal schedule. For example, I'm a night owl, so my tank lights come on at 3:00 P.M. and go off at 3:00 A.M.

To summarize, reef tank lighting should be very intense, and should have a spectral output in the 5500K range.

Metal halide lighting is the best choice, although satisfactory results can be obtained with fluorescent lamps, if enough of the right kind of lamps are used.

Lamps should be on for 12 hours a day, preferably regulated by a timer.

Always take every precaution to insure that your lighting system is installed and operated safely.

Chapter Four

Live Rock

The introduction of live rock represents the arrival of the first living organisms (except nitrifying bacteria, of course) in your reef aquarium.

As we saw in Chapter Three, "cycling" your reef tank involves the establishment of a large population of beneficial nitrifying bacteria in the filter.

Since you need a large population of these organisms, you begin the cycling process with a relatively high concentration of ammonia (approx. 3 ppm) in the system.

When the process is complete, there will be an equally high concentration of nitrate present.

Furthermore, since the conversion of ammonia to nitrite and subsequently to nitrate liberates acid (hydrogen ions), the pH of the water may be less than 8.2, and at least some of the carbonate hardness (alkalinity) will have been neutralized by the acid.

To correct these conditions, it is necessary to drain the system and replace all of the water, or at least to do a major partial water change.

You should check pH, nitrates, alkalinity and specific gravity at this point, and use the results of these tests to guide you in determining how much water to change. If you want to be certain that nothing is amiss, change 100 percent of the water in the system.

Remember to use a high quality salt mix, and the purest freshwater you can obtain or prepare. (See Chapter Two for water treatment techniques.) Once this step is completed, you are ready to begin construction of your living reef.

What is "live rock"? Simply put, live rock is chunks of rock taken from the ocean with various species of encrusting organisms attached.

Having said this, however, it is important to recognize that many, many types of material are available, and there is great variation among them, both in terms of quality, and in terms of their suitability for the reef aquarium.

Live rock may vary as to the geological nature of the rock itself, the depth from which it is collected, prevailing water conditions at the time of collection, and the care (or lack thereof) with which the collector chooses specimens.

In addition, of course, the types of organisms present may vary greatly from one piece of rock to another. Let's consider the characteristics of good quality live rock.

For purposes of this discussion we will classify all live rock into two types: base rock, intended for constructing the base, or wall, of the reef aquarium; and decorative rock, which most aquarists add to the tank for its interest and aesthetic appeal.

First, let's consider the geological nature of the rock.

Ideally, one wants a porous, relatively less dense material. Such rock will contain numerous pores, holes and cavities which harbor not only live invertebrates, macroalgae and their larvae and spores, but also large numbers of beneficial nitrifying bacteria.

The interior of such specimens can also be expected to contain anaerobic, denitrifying bacteria. These will assist in the removal of nitrates from the aquarium and are thus also beneficial.

The best quality base rock is collected in moderately deep water, and consists largely of old, dead coral heads or coral rock rubble that has been broken up by surf or storms, and subsequently colonized by invertebrates and macroalgae. The bulk of this material is imported from various Pacific islands and the Sea of Cortez.

Because of the great shipping distance, such material tends to be costly, but it is well worth the investment for the aquarist seeking the very best quality material for the reef tank.

As a bonus, this type of base rock is less dense than other types, so a given weight of rock will occupy more tank volume.

The Caribbean is the source for another good quality base rock. Its geological origin is largely volcanic. This makes Caribbean base rock more dense, but still affords plenty of cavities and pores.

Like its Pacific counterpart, Caribbean base rock is highly irregular in shape, and thus lends itself to construction of an open, complex reef structure with plenty of caves, nooks and ledges to receive corals and other invertebrates that will be placed upon it.

Base rock from Florida sources can be highly variable in quality. This material is formed from either Miami limestone or Key Largo limestone.

Miami limestone is a fine grained material, usually gray in color, formed around 100,000 years ago from sediments.

Key Largo limestone is the fossil remains of ancient coral reefs that were present in the area now called Florida, again about 100,000 years ago. Key Largo limestone is more porous in structure, and therefore more desirable than the more compact Miami limestone.

Much Florida base rock is collected in shallow water, meaning that the organisms, such as macroalgae and invertebrates, that are present on such rocks can be expected to be extremely hardy species.

This is, of course, desirable. On the downside, however, even the best Florida base rock tends to be somewhat uniform in shape, consisting of oblong, rounded pieces.

Beware of material with sharp, angular edges that is touted as base rock. This is usually chunks of Key Largo limestone (quarried by the ton throughout the Florida Keys) used in road construction.

When this material is dumped at the edge of the sea, in the course of bridge construction, for example, it rapidly becomes colonized by tree oysters, crumb-of-bread sponge and filamentous algae.

None of these are particularly desirable for the reef tank, and many times the oysters die, posing a potential pollution problem. Also, beware of rock heavily coated with silt.

Some debris is to be expected, but a thick coating of fine, silty mud with a modeling clay consistency usually indicates that the rock was taken from very calm, shallow water. In the Florida Keys, such locations are apt to be badly polluted.

While organisms growing on such rock may prove to be extremely hardy, rock taken from polluted waters may even pose a health hazard to the aquarist, not to mention the tank!

For the hobbyist on a limited budget, Florida base rock may be the only affordable option, as the price tends to be less than that of rock from other locations. Use of Florida base, if the material is of good quality as described above, is in no way detrimental.

However, there are better, albeit more expensive, alternatives.

All live rock must be "cured" before it is ready for use. Some suppliers cure the rock for you, and some do not. Because of the time and mess involved in the curing process, cured rock will be more expensive than uncured rock of the same type.

Just what do I mean by "curing?" To answer this fully, let's consider how live rock is collected and transported to your dealer.

Most collectors work in relatively shallow water, using snorkel or SCUBA equipment, bringing up as many chunks of rock as they can carry, and storing them in tubs or baskets on the deck of the dive boat. Hopefully, they are kept covered by wet blankets or tarps to prevent drying under the harsh tropical sun.

When the boat returns from a collecting excursion, the rock is packed in boxes, usually surrounded by wet newspaper, and shipped via air freight to the dealer. Many organisms that were originally present on the rock are, surprisingly, able to survive his process.

Others, however, are not so hardy. This latter group of organisms, which includes various species of sponges, especially, cannot endure the rigors of such a journey, and thus die.

The die-off of these organisms has several effects when the rock is once again placed in water upon arrival at its destination.

First, the decay process releases large quantities of ammonia into the system, taxing the biological filter.

Second, huge amounts of organic matter are released, making the protein skimmer work overtime. Shiny, white, toothpaste-like growths of bacteria and fungi spread over the dead areas of the rock.

As if all this were not enough, the decay bacteria produce hydrogen sulfide, which escapes from the tank and fills the air with the pervasive smell of an open sewer line.

The process of curing live rock simply involves allowing this die-off and decay process to occur under controlled conditions in special holding vats, rather than having it occur in the display tank.

Freshly shipped rock is first rinsed in seawater to remove sediment, and any obviously dead or dying organisms are removed by hand.

The rock is then placed in holding tanks for a period of one week. At the end of that time, areas of decay will be apparent, and large decay spots are siphoned off, or removed with a brush.

The rock specimens are then transferred to the second stage holding tanks, after another good rinsing in seawater, and are held there for an additional week or more.

The end result is clean rock with a full complement of desirable marine life still intact, but without dead or dying sponges, etc., that would pollute the display tank.

If you choose to cure your own live rock, I suggest you do so in a container separate from your new reef tank, unless you are prepared to remove all the rock after a couple of weeks, siphon out all the accumulated debris, change the activated carbon, clean any mechanical filters and/or prefilters, and carry out a 100 percent water change.

Also, be prepared to have your tank smell like a sewer for at least a week or two.

The end result may be much the same as if you had purchased cured rock, but most aquarists are just not prepared for all the hassles involved.

How much base rock will you need? This is hard to answer, since the weight of a given volume of rock may vary greatly.

For example, top quality Pacific rock often weighs only about half as much as a similar sized piece of good quality Florida base. With this in mind, allow about one pound of rock per gallon of tank capacity, if you are using the Pacific material, and 1.5-2 pounds per gallon if using Florida rock.

Should all the rock be added at once? This depends upon whether you are using cured or uncured rock. Cured rock may be added in any amount, at any time, since it will not produce pollutants that can harm specimens already in the tank.

On the other hand, uncured rock, if used at all, must all be added at once.

This is because the cycle of die-off and pollution described earlier would pose a threat to any organisms already living in the tank.

Of course, if you are adding only base rock, you could do so in several batches, but wait until the final batch is cured and the tank has been broken down and cleaned thoroughly before adding any of the more delicate species of invertebrates.

Finally, it should be obvious from the foregoing discussion that one should never, ever introduce a piece of uncured live rock into an established reef tank housing corals, anemones and other delicate species.

We have compared the merits of cured versus uncured live rock, and discussed the selection of base rock.

Base rock is used to construct the "foundation" of your reef tank, forming a support for the corals and other invertebrates that you will later be adding.

Base rock also contributes beneficial bacteria, as well as the larval forms of other organisms that will eventually make their appearance, giving the reef tank that desirable "natural" look.

The very best type of base rock is material from the western Pacific that has been "cured" by the dealer before you add it to the tank. While such top quality base rock is expensive, you will need only about half as much, about one pound per gallon, as you will need of any other type of base rock.

Let's assume that you have placed the appropriate amount of base rock in your reef tank, and that you are ready to add other organisms.

At this point, consider filling in the reef structure you have built with some of the other types of cured live rock that are available. In this way, you will create a truly natural and appropriate setting for the sponges, corals, anemones, tube worms, crustaceans, mollusks and fish that you will be placing in the tank.

There are at least six types of cured live rock available for decorating the reef tank :

These are:

• plant rock, both collected and tank-raised;
• false coral rock, upon which the dominant organism is Florida false coral (*Ricordea florida*);
• zoanthid rock, dominated by various species of *zoanthids* (sea mat) depending upon the source;
• plume or "koko" worm rock, which consists of *Porites* coral heads embedded with colonies of serpulid worms;
• the very similar Christmas tree worm rock;
• and "decorative live rock," a catch-all category including any interesting rock specimen collected with a full complement of encrusting organisms.

Let's consider each of these types of live rock in relation to their use in the reef tank.

✔ Plant rock is simply live rock upon which one or more species of macroalgae predominates. There may, of course, be additional organisms present on the rock, but plants are the primary colonizer. Such material generally does not come from the reef itself.

While certain macroalgae are found on reefs, plant rock available to aquarists is most often collected in shallow, back reef areas, where the absence of herbivorous fishes permits many types of seaweeds to flourish. Many aquarists nevertheless include macroalgae in the reef tank for a variety of good reasons.

Macroalgae add a desirable, natural appearance to the tank. Their varied forms and shades of green create a pleasing scene, and macroalgae absorb ammonia and other nitrogenous compounds, reducing the load on the biological filter.

By absorbing carbon dioxide and releasing oxygen, macroalgae also help to maintain a high pH in the aquarium, and increase the redox potential.

The presence of a good growth of macroalgae also helps to inhibit the growth of undesirable hair and slime algae, the "weeds" of the reef tank.

On the downside, macroalgae, at least some species, can be devilishly tricky to grow. Many fishes—tangs, angels, and several others—will feed heavily on macroalgae, making such fishes unsuitable for a tank in which macroalgae are to be grown.

On occasion, a lush growth of macroalgae will experience a massive die-off, due to nutrient depletion or other

factors. In the event this happens, high levels of pollutants can be released into the tank.

Despite these drawbacks, many aquarists add
macroalgae to their reef aquariums, and there is no
denying that such displays are very attractive. If you
wish to include marine "plants" in your reef tank, by all
means, do so.

Introducing macroalgae via plant rock is one of the best
ways to establish these species in the aquarium.

Collected plant rock is sometimes available with healthy
growths of *Caulerpa* present. More often, however,
species such as *Dictyosphaerium*, *Valonia* or *Codium* are
present.

Calcareous macroalgae such as *Udotea*, *Penicillus* and
Halimeda often do best if obtained attached to plant
rock. Many other species of macro-algae may be found
on collected plant rock, and these vary considerably in
their suitability for the aquarium.

The aquarist can spend many fascinating hours in establishing a tank devoted primarily to the culture of
macroalgae, and such a project is to be encouraged.

A macroalgae tank can contain many organisms besides
the algae themselves: seahorses, slugs, and certain
anemones, that are found in heavily vegetated, shallow
water marine habitats.

✔ Tank raised plant rock has been made available by
Frank Hoff of Florida Aqua Farms. This company has
been a pioneer in the marine aquaculture industry,
especially with regard to high quality tank-raised
macroalgae.

With the introduction of tank-raised plant rock, Mr. Hoff has created a product sure to win ready acceptance.

Most tank-raised plant rock has one or more species of *Caulerpa* present. In my experience, these *Caulerpa* specimens are much easier to grow than loose *Caulerpa* which must be "trained" upon a suitable substrate.

Tank-raised plant rock ships well, is easy to grow, and is priced reasonably. Further, this material is free of the heavy sediments and potential pathogens that may be present on collected plant rock.

✔ *Zoanthid* rock comes from both Atlantic and Pacific ocean reef sources.

This material, mostly collected from shallow water, is dominated by the presence of one or (rarely) more than one, species of zoanthid, or "sea mat."

By far the most commonly available specimens are colonies of the green sea mat, *Zoanthus sociatus*, from Florida and the Caribbean. Less commonly seen are golden sea mat, *Palythoa* sp. and *Isaurus duchassaingi*, a related species.

From Hawaii, seven species of sea mats may be available. The most attractive is *Isaurus elongatus* which has polyps about two inches in length. In *Isaurus*, the dime-sized crown of tentacles is usually a lovely greenish-blue color.

Palythoa vestitus, *P. psammophilia*, *P. toxica*, *Zoanthus pacificus* and *Z. kealakekuanensis* are also found on Hawaiian live rock specimens.

All sea mats do well in the aquarium, provided they receive adequate light.

Living as they do in shallow waters, the sea mats require bright light. They are otherwise hardy and undemanding.

Specimens of *Zoanthus* are often heavily laden with fine silt, and should be rinsed in seawater to remove as much silt as possible before being placed in the reef tank.

Other zoanthids, including *Palythoa caribaea*, *P. tuberculosa*, *Parazoanthus axinellae* and *P. swifti*, are deep-reef organisms and thus are rarely found on sea mat rock from shallow water.

These species do, however, appear on decorative live rock from the deep reef, and make good aquarium inhabitants. Sea mats are among the most easily kept reef invertebrates.

✔ Florida false coral (*Ricordea florida*) is a favorite species. Like the mushroom polyps imported from the Pacific, *Ricordea* polyps are flattened disks, averaging about an inch in diameter, that occur in scattered colonies in waters up to 60 feet down.

The tentacles are round knobs about 1/16" across, and are usually bright blue green in color, although rarely specimens are orange, pink or blue-gray in color. The more green pigment present in a given specimen, the greater the likelihood that it came from shallow water.

Give *Ricordea* plenty of light. It is a true reef organism, and will thrive in the aquarium. False coral rock is seldom available, but makes a striking addition to the reef tank. Like other mushroom polyps, it is easy to keep.

✔ Worm rocks are collected from both the Atlantic and Pacific Oceans. Pacific material is most often chunks of Porites coral, in which are embedded several to many calcareous tubes of the annelid worm *Spirobranchus*. The radioles, or feeding tentacles, of this species come in every color except pink, with blue being predominant.

✔ A larger worm, usually found singly or in small colonies of two or three individuals, is collected in the Caribbean. This is sold under the name "Christmas tree worm rock." Caribbean specimens are rarely associated with *Porites* coral, and come in all colors, but blue specimens are quite rare.

Nevertheless, both Pacific plume rock and Caribbean Christmas tree worm rock are classified as *Spirobranchus giganteus*.

Easy to keep and very colorful, neither should be housed in a tank with angelfishes. Dwarf angels of the genus *Centropyge*, especially, are prone to extracting the worms from their tubes and eating them.

Most other types of live rock are sold by the pound. Plume and Christmas tree worm rocks are usually sold by the piece, with the price being determined by the number of worms present and their colors.

Unusually dense colonies, or specimens that contain unusually strikingly colored worms, may command a high price. Rocks bearing colonies of other species of serpulid worms, which often have bright red radioles, are occasionally available. All these worms are long-lived in the aquarium.

Since they do not possess symbiotic algae, the worms are indifferent to lighting conditions, and require regular feedings. Coralife Target Food, Coral Nutrient and Roti-Rich are excellent foods for serpulid worms of all types.

Having said all this, I must urge you not to consider purchasing the Pacific "plume" rock type of worm rock.

Here is why.

Tropical coral reefs provide all of the specimens that marine aquarists keep in their tanks. It is important to protect and conserve reef life, in order that there will always be a supply of fishes, invertebrates and marine plants for us to enjoy as hobbyists.

Many coral reefs have suffered severe damage from pollution, development, destructive fishing practices such as cyanide and dynamite, and collection of curios (e.g., "decorative" corals).

As aquarists, we have a responsibility to the reef, for without it, our hobby could not exist. This is why responsible dealers no longer sell "plume" or "koko" worm rocks.

These specimens are broken from the reef structure itself, damaging the delicate *Porites* coral in which the worms are embedded. Many of the worm tubes themselves are broken in half during collection, killing the worms, or at best leaving them behind in a damaged condition.

The *Porites* coral surrounding the worms invariably dies in captivity, and the resulting coral skeleton becomes an ideal site for colonization by undesirable hair and slime algae in the aquarium.

I urge all aquarists to become involved in reef conservation. One way you can do this is to refuse to purchase specimens collected in a manner that damages reef habitats, such as "plume" and "koko" worm rocks.

If you would like more information about what you can do to help conserve coral reefs, write to the International Marinelife Alliance, 2883 Otterson Drive, Ottawa, Ontario K1V 7B2, Canada, or contact your state's chapter of The Nature Conservancy.

Many species of invertebrates encrust rocky substrates, and "decorative live rock," sometimes called "deco rock," may harbor a selection of these.

This material may vary greatly, depending upon where and how it was collected and cured.

The best quality cured deco rock will have a variety of colorful organisms present, and no two pieces will be quite alike. This material is most often priced by the piece, with $100 or more per piece not an unheard-of price.

One or two pieces of good deco rock can be used as the centerpiece of a reef tank, however, and will reward the owner with a myriad of fascinating invertebrates in a variety of forms and colors.

Any of the organisms already mentioned may occur on deco rock, along with small coral colonies, *gorgonians*, and, especially, a variety of multi-colored *sponges* and *bryozoans*. When properly collected and cured, deco rock can be the most interesting specimen in the reef tank.

All types of live rock are hardy. Their primary requirements are good water quality and, where appropriate, adequate light. Feeding with Coralife products, Coral Nutrient and Roti-Rich is recommended, but add these foods very sparingly.

With such care, all types of live rock should improve in

appearance with time, even in the smallest reef tank.
Some of the organisms that may be found on live rock
belong to taxonomic groups that will be encountered
nowhere else in the aquarium trade.

I shall mention each of these minor groups here, since
many aquarists want to know what is living on the live
rock specimens that they place in the tank.

Very brief descriptions of each group are included.

✔ Sponges. Large, colorful sponges are often imported
for the aquarium, and do very well in the reef tank. Live
rock specimens may harbor a variety of sponges, in an
array of colors.

Many have interesting patterns of growth, with some
actually boring into the structure of the rock itself.

Sponges are mentioned here, because they can be distinguished from the remainder of the organisms listed
by virtue of their porous structure, and the absence of
tentacles of any kind.

✔ *Annelids* and Other Worms. In addition to embedded
fanworms of various types, the worm fauna of live rock
may include *cirratulids*, which are annelids with long,
spaghetti-like tentacles, and a bewildering variety of
motile annelids with scales, spines, and bristles.

Only large or numerous bristleworms pose any threat of
harm to other reef tank organisms.

Minor worm groups found, usually within crevices, on
live rock include *sipunculids*, also called peanut-worms,
and the rare *echiurids*. The *sipunculids* are usually drab
in color, and have a long, extensible proboscis.

Echiurids are often brown or gray, but occasionally are lavender, pale green, or other pastel shades, and may be distinguished by the flattened, triangular proboscis. *Sipunculids* and *echiurids* are detritis feeders.

Nemertean worms are flattened, ribbon-like, and very elongated. They may be variously colored and patterned. Nemerteans feed on small invertebrates, but pose no threat to the inhabitants of the reef tank.

Flatworms may also be quite colorful, and can be recognized by their smooth, very flattened bodies. They are seldom more than and inch or two in length.

Most flatworms are predatory, and feed on other invertebrates.

If you find one, observe it closely to determine its feeding preferences, and remove it from the tank only if it seems to have a taste for something desirable.

✔ Bryozoans. The bryozoans are all colonial, and many resemble plants. In fact, the name "bryozoan" means "moss animal".

These are filter feeders that may encrust large areas of live rock, forming colonies that are often rather stiff and hard, owing to a skeletal structure composed of calcium carbonate, or tough protein material.

They can be recognized by a circle of tentacles that is just visible to the naked eye, and appears much like a tiny fanworm. Most are quite colorful.

✔ *Tunicates*. Many species of colonial *tunicates* may be found on live rock specimens.

They are beautiful animals, usually colorful, and quite

delicate-looking, appearing to be constructed of translucent glass.

Larger *tunicates*, about the size of a grape or marble, can clearly be seen to possess a pair of body openings, side-by-side.

Water is drawn into one of these, the food material is strained out, and the water is expelled through the other opening.

Consult field guides, or a good book on marine invertebrates, for pictures of each of these groups of live rock organisms.

Chapter Five

Water Analysis and Routine Maintenance

How's your water quality? In order to successfully maintain marine fish and invertebrates in the aquarium for
any length of time, it is important that we provide them
with water conditions similar to those that they are
accustomed to in nature.

To assure that these conditions are met, we need to test
various water quality parameters from time to time, and
take steps to adjust these parameters as required.

In this chapter I will discuss the various tests that you
should perform, what the results mean, and how to
correct problems that you may discover.

✔ Specific gravity.

This is an indirect measurement of the quantity of
dissolved salts in the water.

Average ocean water has a salinity of 35 o/oo, or 35
parts dissolved salts per 1000 parts water. This corre-
sponds to a specific gravity reading of 1.0240 at a

temperature of 75 degrees. This is the hydrometer reading you should be using if you are keeping invertebrates.

Fish are often kept at a lower specific gravity, usually 1.0220, in the belief that the lowered salinity this represents reduces stress on the fishes and makes the survival of parasites more unlikely.

I have never seen objective evidence to support this practice.

Maintaining a constant specific gravity reading usually entails adding fresh water to the tank to compensate for evaporation. You should make sure that this water is of good quality, in order to avoid the introduction of harmful compounds that may build up in the tank over time.

Reverse osmosis units produce purified water for only pennies per gallon.

These units are a wise investment. Copper, phosphates and nitrates can be introduced into the aquarium via tap water. More about these compounds below.

✔ Nitrogen compounds.

Every reef aquarist should be familiar with the process of biological filtration. Ammonia, which is excreted by fish and invertebrates, is converted first to nitrite, and then to nitrate, through the metabolism of nitrifying bacteria.

Ammonia and nitrite are highly toxic to aquatic organisms, while nitrate is less so.

Biological filtration consumes oxygen, and produces acidic compounds as a by-product. Both these facts are important in terms of the overall water quality of the tank. You should test your tank every week for the accumulation of nitrate.

Tests for both ammonia and nitrite need not be carried out routinely, but check both promptly if there is any reason to suspect a problem is developing in the tank. The test for either compound should always be zero.

If either ammonia or nitrite is detected in the tank, do a partial water change immediately, and make an effort to determine what has affected the biological filter.

Some common causes of this kind of problem are: too many animals in the tank, uneaten food or a dead animal is decaying in the tank, the filter is receiving insufficient oxygen, the bacteria in the filter system have been weakened or killed, or some combination of these.

Unfortunately, there is no "quick fix" should the nitrifying bacteria die for some reason. These bacteria are relatively slow growing, and if you lose them, it may take up to a month for the filtration system to recover.

Therefore, one of the most important aspects of aquarium maintenance is to make sure that none of the problems described above has a chance to occur.

Nitrates, ideally, should be at zero concentration in the reef tank. In any case maintain nitrate levels below 10 mg/l. This can be accomplished via regular partial water changes, the use of a denitrification filter, or the use of nitrate removing resins and compounds.

Fish are more tolerant of nitrates, and the level in a fish-only tank can be allowed to reach 40 mg/l before corrective measures must be taken. Tangs, however, may stop eating if nitrates exceed 20 mg/l.

Confusion exists among many hobbyists concerning the interpretation of test results for ammonia, nitrite, and nitrate.

This confusion has arisen because there are two ways of expressing the concentrations of these substances, and because some test kit manufacturers do not bother to point out this information on their packaging.

Concentration of NH_3, NO_2^- and NO_3^- may be expressed either as the concentration of the ion or as the concentration of nitrogen in ionic form.

Note that nitrogen (N) appears in the chemical formulas for each of these compounds:

ammonia NH_3 - one atom of nitrogen, 3 atoms of hydrogen; nitrite NO_2^- - one atom of nitrogen, 2 atoms of oxygen; nitrate NO_3^- - one atom of nitrogen, 3 atoms of oxygen.

Each of these contains nitrogen, but each is different from the others because of the additional atoms (oxygen or hydrogen) present.

We generally are interested in the ion concentrations, but knowing the nitrogen concentration is useful, too, and making the conversion from one to the other is a matter of simple arithmetic.

Some test kits for ammonia, nitrite and nitrate measure the ion concentration, and some measure nitrogen.

It's important to know the difference when comparing readings taken with two different test kits.

Here's how to do it:

If your test kit measures:

Total Ammonia (NH_3+NH_4+) Divide by 1.3 to obtain ammonia nitrogen (NH_4+-N)

Nitrite Ion (NO_2-) Divide by 3.3 to obtain nitrite nitrogen (NO_2—N)

Nitrate Ion (NO_3-) Divide by 4.4 to obtain nitrate nitrogen (NO_3—N)

To convert nitrogen readings to ion equivalents, multiply by the appropriate number from the list above.

Ion equivalents are important when you are concerned about the toxicity of the compound.

Nitrogen equivalents allow you to make comparisons among the concentrations of these compounds, to assess filter efficiency, for example.

The accuracy of different brands of test kits may vary quite surprisingly, and, as mentioned earlier, some manufacturers do not bother to explain how to make the conversions discussed above.

I have personally evaluated three brands of nitrate test kits, both for accuracy in measurement, and for the quality of information provided on the package inserts.

This was done simply by testing the same tank with each kit, following label directions.

Here are the results of that evaluation:

(For comparison, all results were converted to NO_3—N in mg/l, rounded the the nearest 1 mg/l.)

Brand	Measures	Result	Cost
A	NO3-	8-9	$ 11.50
B	NO3—N	7	15.00
C	NO3-	32	9.00

Note that the cheapest test kit gave about four times the reading of the other two. This kit also provided no information about converting from ion to nitrogen readings.

Independent, professional laboratory analysis of the same water sample yielded a value of 8.1 mg/l.

I repeated this comparison, using new kits of each of the three brands, and again had the same sample analyzed professionally. The results were:

Brand	Reading(NO-3-N)
A	4
B	25
C	>32

Lab (Method 1)	6.3
(Method 2)	5.7

Note that the professional analysis was done by two different methods. This is one way of cross-checking the accuracy of laboratory analyses.

From these results, one can draw several conclusions:

1. Brand A is the most accurate test, and was consistently accurate.

2. Brand B gave reasonably accurate results in the first series of tests, but was way off on the second series. (I found this surprising, and even repeated the second test twice to make certain the error was not due to my own ineptitude.)

Since two different Brand B test kits were used for the two separate series of tests, this finding suggests Brand B kits may give widely varying results from one batch of kits to the next.

3. Brand C kits were consistently inaccurate, giving a reading 4 to 5 times higher than the actual concentration.

If you have doubts about the accuracy of the test kits you are using, have them checked against a known analysis by a professional.

✔ pH.

The degree of acidity or alkalinity of the aquarium is referred to as pH. Reef tanks should be kept at a pH of 8.2 to 8.3, which is alkaline.

Owing to the production of acidic compounds by the biological filtration process, and the release of various acidic products by the metabolism of fishes and invertebrates, the natural tendency is for the pH of any aquarium to decline over a period of time.

In no case should the pH of a reef tank be allowed to drop below 7.8. Test pH weekly.

If it is found to be below 8.0, test the alkalinity (see

below). If the alkalinity is greater than 2.5 meq/l, check for the build up of carbon dioxide in the tank. This can be done by removing a couple of gallons of water and aerating it vigorously overnight.

Then test the pH of the aerated water and compare this to the pH of the tank. If the pH of the aerated water is measurably higher than that of the tank, carbon dioxide is accumulating in the aquarium.

This can be corrected by increasing aeration in the tank, removing some animals, or both. (This tip came from Sea Scope, published by Aquarium Systems, Inc.)

✔ Alkalinity.

Known by various names, KH, carbonate hardness, etc., this is a measure of the buffering capacity of the water, and is expressed in milli-equivalents per liter (meq/l).

Buffering capacity refers to the ability of the water to resist changes in pH when acid is added. A reading of 2.5 - 5.0 meq/l is considered to be the proper range. Always check alkalinity when the pH is found to be lower than normal (see above).

Additions of buffering compounds can be used to increase the alkalinity. Partial water changes will also help to accomplish this.

The use of carbonate substrates, such as crushed coral, crushed shell, etc., is erroneously believed to be of assistance in maintaining pH. In fact, these materials can actually LOWER alkalinity, by encouraging the precipitation of calcium carbonate from the water.

In addition, phosphates (see below) accumulate in the tank more readily when such materials are used. Most authors now recommend using silica sand as a substrate, or better yet, no substrate at all.

Eventually, coralline algae and other organisms will encrust the bottom of the tank, hiding the glass.

If you must use substrate in a tank with wet/dry filtration, only about 1/4 inch of substrate should be used.

✔ Dissolved Oxygen.

Seawater at 75 degrees will contain about 6.8 mg/l of dissolved oxygen at 100% saturation. You should have sufficient aeration to achieve this concentration or higher, as levels of 125% saturation can occur in the reef environment.

Every living organism in the tank, from the nitrifying, bacteria to the fish, requires oxygen to sustain life. Oxygen depletion, even slightly below saturation, can create stress for fish and invertebrates.

Check the dissolved oxygen concentration (D.O.) when the tank is first set up, and each time new specimens are added (wait about 24 hours after adding new animals before checking D.O.).

A test now available to aquarists, marketed by Precision Aquarium Testing (P.A.T.), Stuart, Florida, greatly simplifies the D.O. test.

Most other tests require careful attention to the collection of the sample, and proper use of several test chemicals, in order to produce an accurate test result.

The P.A.T.test is carried out in one step, in the tank itself, and costs about $2.50 per test.

✔ Copper.

Copper has long been used in the treatment of the common parasitic diseases of marine fish. Its importance to the reef aquarist has to do with the quality of tap water used to make seawater for the aquarium.

If the tap water is held in copper tanks, or flows through copper pipes, enough copper may find its way into the tank to accumulate to toxic levels over a period of time.

This usually happens when tap water is added to the tank frequently to compensate for evaporation, coupled with infrequent water changes.

Even though only a trace of copper may be present in the tap water, after several months it accumulates and causes problems.

Using distilled water from the grocery may not solve the problem, since steam distilled water is often produced in copper vessels.

A reverse osmosis unit will remove copper, as will Poly-Filter™.

 If you've been adding tap water to the tank and not doing water changes, and are now experiencing problems with invertebrates, check the tank for copper. The level should always be zero. If it isn't, do a major water change immediately, and take steps to eliminate the source of the copper.

✔ Iron.

This element is essential for macroalgae, as well as for fish and invertebrates. Animals can get the iron they need from the foods they eat, but macroalgae, such as

Caulerpa, must absorb iron from the water surrounding them.

Unfortunately, iron is difficult to keep in solution at the pH of the marine tank. Therefore, it is usually necessary to add an iron supplement, such as Coralife Macroalgae Iron Supplement, to the water. Thiel Aqua Tech make a similar supplement called Macro-algae fertilizer.

The iron levels of the marine tank should be 0.05 - 0.1 mg/l. Before beginning the use of an iron supplement, check the tank to determine the iron content. Then add supplement, a little at a time, retesting periodically, until 0.1 mg/l is reached.

Make a note of the time. Wait twenty-four hours and test for iron again. It will be less than 0.1 mg/l. Again add iron supplement until the 0.1 mg/l level is restored, keeping track of the amount of supplement you have added.

This is the amount you will need to add daily to maintain the desired level of iron in the tank. Retest for iron periodically, since the amount used up by the tank's inhabitants may change as they grow or as new specimens are added.

Iron supplementation is necessary only for reef tanks with macroalgae. Otherwise, no supplementation, and no iron test, is needed.

Make sure that the supplement you use contains iron in "chelated" form, and that it does not also contain phosphates.

Chelation is usually achieved by means of EDTA, or similar chemicals.

🖎 Phosphates.

Compounds containing phosphorous and oxygen are called phosphates, and occur in all living organisms.

Thus, phosphates find their way into the aquarium water as a result of various biological process that occur in the tank.

They may also be introduced via the tap water, or in some synthetic seawater mixes, and in some tank additives.

Accumulation of phosphates is generally regarded to be one of the major contributing factors in the annoyingly over-luxuriant growth of filamentous and slime algae that plague marine aquarists. If you have an algae problem, test for phosphates.

If the test shows any measurable level of phosphate (about 0.05 mg/l is the lower limit for most phosphate test kits), start looking for ways to reduce the phosphate concentration in the tank.

This is not easy to do.

First, check your tap water; if you are using a reverse osmosis unit, check this water also, to make sure the unit is removing phosphates. Mix up some fresh synthetic seawater. Test this for phosphates; many brands contain them.

Mix up a bucket of water with the appropriate dose of the buffering compound you are using and test it. Many buffers rely on phosphate compounds to generate their effects.

If you are using a carbonate gravel, consider replacing

it with silica, or using no gravel at all (see recommendations by various authors such as Sprung and Thiel).

Clean your filter system regularly, as accumulations of detritus may contain very high phosphate concentrations.

All of these measures will help to combat algae growth in the tank. Two products remove phosphates from the tank, these are Poly-Filter™ and X-Phosphate™.

Using these in addition to the other steps outlined above will help to keep the tank's phosphate content as low as possible.

As more aquarists become aware of the role of phosphates in the development of algae blooms in the marine aquarium, perhaps more manufacturers will begin producing salt mixes, buffers, and other products that do not contain phosphates, and will advertise this fact for the benefit of aquarists.

One final note about testing for phosphates. Purchase a supply of disposable plastic vials in which to carry out phosphate tests.

Your dealer, druggist, or a chemical supply house should carry these. Use a fresh vial for each test.

Phosphates are difficult to remove from such containers, and can build up and result in spurious test results.

✔ General Recommendations.

Keep a record of all water tests that you carry out, and include the date, and any comments you deem important. In this way you will develop a history of conditions in your tank that can be of great value in diagnosing problems that crop up. Such a log can also help you to spot trends in water quality fluctuations, enabling you to take corrective action before such fluctuations become serious.

Buy good quality test kits and follow the instructions provided by the manufacturer.

✔ Summary.

Test your tank periodically and keep records of the results.

The tests you should be performing, and the results you should get are listed in Table 5-1.

TABLE 5-1

Water Quality Parameters for Reef Aquariums

Parameter	Desired Reading
specific gravity	1.0240
temperature	75 degrees
ammonia	0 mg/l
nitrite	0 mg/l
nitrate (ion)	<10 mg/l
pH	8.2 - 8.3
alkalinity	2.5 - 5.0 meq/l
dissolved oxygen	>6.8 mg/l
copper	0 mg/l
iron	0.05 - 0.1 mg/l
phosphate	<0.05 mg/l
redox potential	350 - 400 mV

Values are suggested only.

Adjust for temperature differences wherever necessary.

✔ Routine Maintenance.

Before we go any further with a discussion of corals, anemones, plants and fishes, I thought it would be wise to cover the topic of routine maintenance.

Maintenance is a chore that no one likes to do, but which is absolutely necessary for long-term success. Begin a maintenance routine while only live rock is present in the tank, so that you will have formed the habit of regular care by the time more delicate organisms are added.

I have organized my recommendations for reef tank care in a series of logical groups, depending upon the frequency with which various tasks should be done.

✔ Recordkeeping.

I cannot emphasize enough the value of keeping a permanent record of your maintenance chores, water changes and observations of the reef tank.

In time, you will develop a "history" of your tank that can help in problem solving, diagnosis of water quality changes over time, and the behavior of the invertebrates and fishes.

One can purchase record books with printed forms for aquarium records, but I just use a simple loose-leaf binder.

As a minimum, record the results of every water test you perform (include both date and time of test), date and amount of water changes, and the name, size and date of introduction of each specimen you place in the tank.

Other important data you can record are such things as

date of lamp replacements, filter media changes, feeding schedules and type of foods preferred, and events such as spawnings or deaths of animals.

If you shop at a number of different aquarium stores, it will be instructive to keep track of which animals came from which store. This practice will help you pinpoint the best source for the species in which you are interested.

The wise aquarist will also record purchase dates for equipment for warranty purposes (staple your receipt to the page, so you will have proof of purchase if a warranty repair or replacement should become necessary).

✔ Water Changes.

As I have said many times before, no filtration system, regardless of its complexity, will eliminate the need for regular partial water changes.

Thus, periodically you will need to remove some water and replace it with freshly prepared synthetic seawater (or natural seawater, if you can obtain it).

How much water should you change and how often should you change it? I have seen recommendations that vary from a gallon or so every day to 100 percent every month.

It doesn't seem to make much difference which schedule you follow, as long as you are consistent.

My personal preference is to change small quantities of water more frequently, perhaps two gallons every three or four days in a 100-gallon tank. The idea behind this approach is to keep fluctuations in overall water quality to a minimum (see also Thiel).

Change at least 20 percent of the tank during the course of every month, no matter what.

In addition to partial water changes, you will need to add water rather frequently to compensate for evaporation. Reef tanks typically lose water to evaporation at a rapid rate.

Therefore, adding make-up water is a significant maintenance chore.

Salinity fluctuations that occur as a result of evaporation, and the subsequent addition of fresh water, can be quite large if you neglect "topping-up" for too long.

For example, consider a tank of 100 gallons (72" x 18" x 18"). Dissolved in the water in this tank are some 13.3 kilograms of salt (at a salinity of 35 0/00).

If we allow one inch of water to evaporate, the same quantity of salt will now be dissolved in 95.6 gallons of water, giving a salinity of 36.6 0/00. This represents a 5 percent increase in salinity, a very large fluctuation compared to the changes that occur in the ocean.

As a general rule, top up the tank with freshwater on a schedule that results in only a gallon or so of freshwater being added per hundred gallons of tank water. This could be every day, or only once or twice a week, depending upon the evaporation rate.

The quality of freshwater used to top up the tank is important. This is because impurities added with the freshwater will gradually accumulate in the tank.

For some substances often present in tap water, this cumulative effect can have disastrous consequences.

Despite the fact that municipal tap water is (supposedly) safe to drink, impurities such as nitrate, phosphate, copper, lead, arsenic, etc. are present whether you are aware of it or not.

Table 5-2 shows an analysis of tap water in my home town, as an average of samples taken daily from July to December 1989.

Most metals are present in quite small amounts; however, in the aquarium, when repeated additions of tap water are made without intervening water changes, the concentrations of various metals gradually increases, and can approach dangerous levels in a surprisingly short time.

Consider a tank of 100 liters, with 10 liters per week being added to compensate for evaporation, and 10 liters per month being changed :

Assuming the copper level (0.012 ppm) in my tap water does not fluctuate significantly, in seven months this hypothetical tank will contain almost 0.05 ppm copper, enough to detect with a copper test kit. (The actual value is 0.0456 ppm.)

My point is that we should pay close attention to the quality of freshwater we add to our reef tanks, using various methods as needed to purify tap water for aquarium use.

You can usually obtain an analysis of your tap water free of charge from your local water company. (This was the source for the information presented in Table 5-2.)

You may be surprised to discover what's going into your tank (and your coffee)!

✔ Cleaning.

Siphon detritus from both the tank and filter on a regular basis, and clean the prefilter pads every week. This will help to control algae, and to eliminate some of the load on the biological filter.

Bacteria which break down detritus produce ammonia in the process, just as do fish and invertebrates.

Purchase a plastic kitchen baster at the grocery and use it to direct a gentle stream of water to dislodge debris that may accumulate in crannies and crevices throughout the tank. Be especially careful to remove debris that has settled on sponges, soft corals and other sedentary invertebrates.

If algae growth occurs in areas where you do not want it, clean this off regularly as well. The new algae control product from Coralife works best if you clean up the tank first, and then add the product to help keep algae growth from returning.

Erythromycin sulfate is also sometimes used in an attempt to control certain types of microalgae. This antibiotic does indeed kill "slime" algae, which are actually a type of photosynthetic bacteria (*Cyanobacteria*). Erythromycin must be used with extreme caution, however, as it is also highly toxic to nitrifying bacteria.

In addition, I have observed that species in two genera of snails commonly used for algae control, *Astraea* and *Turbo*, are killed by this antibiotic.

Clean up salt accumulations from spray and splattering as soon as you notice it, especially from electrical equipment such as light fixtures and pump housings.

Keep the area around the tank, equipment and cabinet free of ordinary dust and dirt, too.

Your aquarium area should be as clean as your kitchen. (I know, I know, I haven't run the dishwasher in three days myself, but you know what I mean.)

Finally, inspect your tank closely every day. Does everything look healthy and thriving? Is the water clear? Do the fish appear active and searching for food? Is all the equipment working properly? Does the skimmer cup need emptying?

You should ask yourself these and other questions every time you pause to spend a few moments enjoying the tank.

TABLE 5-2

Analysis of Composites of Daily Samples of Raw & Tap Water
July - December 1989
All figures ppm except as noted.

Tap Water	Average
pH	7.7
Alkalinity as CaCO3	68.0
Aluminum (ppb)	105.2
Arsenic (ppb)	<2.0
Cadmium (ppb)	<5.0
Copper (ppb)	12.0
Iron (ppb)	17.0
Lead (ppb)	<2.0
Nickel (ppb)	<5.0
Silica	3.0
Zinc (ppb)	20.0
Nitrates as N (ppm)	1.43
Phosphate (total)	0.10

Chapter Six

Advanced Techniques

So far, we have covered how to set up and care for a reef tank that employed only "essential" equipment, i.e., a basic system that would, with appropriate testing, maintenance and wise selection of specimens, offer the average hobbyist a high likelihood of success.

Presumably many of you who are reading these words will create a reef system aquarium according to the guidelines I have presented, and I hope you enjoy the fruits of your efforts.

You have no doubt surmised that a significant amount of time must be spent in carrying out routine maintenance chores related to your reef aquarium. We all lead busy lives, it seems, and saving time has become as important as saving money.

With that in mind, I will devote this chapter to a discussion of the application of some advanced equipment for the reef tank.

Most of these devices are employed, not with the aim of improving tank conditions, per se, but rather with the aim of making the maintenance of good tank conditions a less time-consuming proposition for the aquarist.

Let us consider, in turn, equipment that will make your life easier in terms of

1) algae control,
2) water handling, and
3) water quality monitoring and maintenance.

✔ Algae Control.

Undesirable growths of microalgae are the bane of reef aquarists. Many authors have devoted many words to this subject, and a plethora of theories have been proposed as to the causes of outbreaks of the these organisms and the means for eliminating them.

In seeking ways to deal with the problem myself over the years, I have noted several factors which seem to be shared by tanks with too much microalgae.

As with many other kinds of problems, the control of microalgae growth in the reef tank requires requires an attack on several levels.

To understand how and why excessive microalgae growth occurs in the aquarium, we must begin by asking why natural reefs do not become overgrown with microalgae.

There appear to be several reasons.

First, on a natural reef much of the space available for colonization by microalgae is already occupied by macroalgae or encrusting animals.

These organisms possess a variety of adaptations to

prevent their living space from being usurped by competing organisms.

This is why I advocate the use of live rock for construction of the entire "reef" within the tank. Some aquarists have chosen to use dead coral rock, lava rock, and similar products to build a reef base, and then add live rock on top.

In my experience, this practice will only encourage colonization of the bare rock surfaces with microalgae that can grow and spread at a much faster rate than any of the organisms present on live rock are able to do.

Thus, before the dead rock material can become encrusted with desirable organisms, microalgae gains a foothold.

A second reason for the lack of microalgae on natural reefs is the abundant presence of herbivorous (algae-eating) animals.

Many species of worms, mollusks, echinoderms, crustaceans and fishes are constantly nibbling away the growths of algae that manage to develop.

Certainly, the addition of some of these organisms to the reef aquarium can benefit in achieving the overall goal of algae control.

Of course, in a tank that contains macroalgae, the selection of herbivores must be a judicious one.

That these two factors, lack of colonization sites and predation by herbivores, can account for the absence of huge mats of microalgae from natural reefs is strongly supported by our observations of what happens when these factors are naturally eliminated.

Certain damselfishes will stake out a particular coral head as their territory, and then systematically kill a portion of the living coral by nipping at the polyps. The dead coral skeleton rapidly becomes colonized with filamentous algae.

The damselfish will vigorously defend its home, driving off intruders much larger than itself, including fishes that would feed on the algae growth.

As a result of this behavior, the damselfish is able to cultivate a private garden of filamentous algae, which it eats, thereby gaining energy and important nutrients without having to stray from the protective confines of the coral head.

Because the damselfish feeds judiciously, and supplements its diet with other organisms, such as plankton that it plucks from the water column, the growth of its garden of microalgae keeps pace with its food requirements.

Here we have a natural analog to an aquarium in which only dead corals and coral rock are used as decorations, and from which herbivores are absent.

But not all aquariums are devoid of live rock and herbivorous animals, and they still experience blooms of microalgae. So other factors must be involved.

As usual, these factors are related to water chemistry, specifically with regard to nutrient ions.

The ocean around natural coral reefs is characterized by very low concentrations of nutrient ions, in contrast to the waters of the sea in many other areas.

Nutrient ions are requisite for the growth of all organisms, including microalgae, and include three chemical species: nitrogen compounds, phosphates, and carbon compounds.

Nitrogen compounds in seawater include mostly ammonia, nitrite, and nitrate.

Marine aquarists have always made every effort to keep ammonia and nitrite concentrations at or near zero, but only recently have they become aware of the importance of keeping nitrate concentrations near zero, as well.

Measured values for total inorganic nitrogen in tropical seas are typically in the range of 1-2 micrograms per liter. That's 1-2 parts per billion for the sum of all ammonia, nitrite, and nitrate present.

For the aquarist using test kits from his or her local shop, this number is effectively zero.

The concentration of phosphorus compounds (measured as dissolved inorganic phosphorus, or orthophosphate) in tropical oceans is even lower than the concentration of nitrate, often only 1-2 parts per 10 billion. Again, read this as "zero" for aquarium purposes.

In the case of carbon compounds, we must consider the various forms in which carbon may be present. Carbon dioxide gas is dissolved in the aquarium water from the atmosphere, and as a result of the respiration of the organisms in the tank.

Carbon is also present in the form of carbonates, ions that participate in the pH buffering system, and which we measure when we perform an alkalinity test.

The third form of carbon is dissolved organic carbon

(D.O.C.), and appears to be a major villain, along with nitrate and phosphate, in contributing to microalgae blooms in the aquarium.

Measuring the level of D.O.C. in seawater is difficult to carry out, but values that have been reported range up to a maximum of about 2 parts per million.

As you may by now have deduced, control of microalgae growth in the aquarium consists primarily in keeping the concentrations of nitrate, phosphate and D.O.C. as close to zero as possible.

Let's consider each of these in turn.

The first step in eliminating phosphate from the aquarium is to introduce as little of it as possible to begin with. This is challenging, since phosphate is ubiquitous in nature.

My city's tap water, for example, contains 0.1 ppm phosphate on an average day. This is about one thousand times the concentration found in tropical ocean water.

Salt mixes, buffers, and various tank additives all may contains phosphates. Select these products from manufacturer's who have made an effort to keep phosphates and nitrates to a minimum without sacrificing overall quality.

If no information is provided on the label, prepare a sample and check it with your phosphate test kit. In the case of foods, you have no choice, since all of necessity will contains phosphates.

This is one reason to feed sparingly and only when warranted by the needs of the organisms in the aquarium.

Much the same can be said of nitrates as was said above regarding phosphates. In addition to all the external sources, foods, additives, etc., the biological filter produces nitrate as an end product. Thus, most of the nitrogen present in the aquarium will end up as nitrate.

Live rock, with its complement of denitrifying bacteria, will help to reduce nitrate somewhat. Performing regular partial water changes will also help to control nitrate concentration, provided, of course, that the replacement water is as free of nitrate as possible.

If you prefer to tinker constantly with a piece of cranky equipment, you can install a denitrifying filter on the tank. These work, but in my opinion are too much trouble.

These same steps will also help lower the phosphate concentration. (There is no "dephosphatizing" filter comparable to a denitrifying filter. If there were, I am sure it would be just as difficult to regulate properly!)

The best answer to the nitrate and phosphate problem is to take all reasonable measures to exclude these ions from the aquarium, and then employ chemical filtration to eliminate the remainder.

Use of chemical filtration constitutes a form of what I will call "post-filtration", i.e., further treatment of the aquarium water after it has passed through the biological filter.

Post-filtration can be used to reduce D.O.C., also. This can be accomplished through the use of activated carbon, as well as chemical media that absorb D.O.C. components.

Chemical filtration media can simply be placed in the

sump of the trickle filter, where water will flow over them.

A much more satisfactory arrangement, however, is to use cartridge filters to contain the media, and to place these between the sump of the trickle filter and the water pump.

Some useful chemical filtration media, and related hardware, include the following. Thiel-Aqua-Tech manufactures cartridge filters for its X-Nitrate and X-Phosphate products, along with a cartridge for Poly-Filter™ disks.

Poly-Bio-Marine also manufacturers a cartridge filter for their Poly-Filter™ discs.

Granular media, such as X-Phosphate, X-Nitrate, and activated carbon, can also be placed in chemical filtration cartridges manufactured by Rainbow Plastics for their Lifeguard™ filters.

All of these are desirable and practical means to employ chemical filtration on your reef tank.

I said above that D.O.C. "apparently" plays a significant role in the promotion of microalgae blooms in the aquarium. I say this because I have observed tanks with heavy growths of microalgae in which the nitrate and phosphate concentrations were acceptably low.

Without speculating as to what the connection might be between D.O.C. and algae growth, I will suggest that the best approach is to keep the concentration of D.O.C. as low as possible.

To accomplish this, several methods must be used simultaneously.

This is because D.O.C. is not one, but many different compounds, and each has different chemical properties.

Methods to reduce D.O.C. include the use of protein skimmers, activated carbon, Poly-Filter™ and other chemical resins, and ozonization.

I mentioned ozone use early in this book because I regard ozone as one of those ideal, but not absolutely essential, components of a good reef system.

Nevertheless, I have come to regard ozone, used in combination with activated carbon, to be one of the most effective ways to control microalgae growth and to reduce D.O.C. in reef aquariums.

Ozone is a highly reactive form of oxygen gas, and a powerful oxidizing agent. To understand how it works in the marine tank, let's start with a little basic chemistry. The processes of oxidation and reduction are chemical concepts that describe what happens when electrons are transferred between atoms.

By definition, reduction is a gain in electrons and oxidation is the loss of electrons. Reducing agents are chemical species that accept electrons, while oxidizing agents are electron donors.

The hydrogen ion (H+) is one of the most frequently encountered reducing agents, while the oxygen ion (O-) is an oxidizing agent. Note that these two processes always occur together.

In other words, in an oxidation-reduction reaction, one of the participating ions becomes oxidized while the other becomes reduced. This is because we are dealing with the transfer of electrons from one atom (ion) to another.

The production of nitrate from ammonia by the biological filter is a good example of a typical oxidation reduction reaction. Ammonia (NH_3) is a reduced form of nitrogen.

In the biological filter it is oxidized to nitrate (NO_3-).

Ozone is capable of oxidizing a wide variety of compounds, and therein lies its major utility to the aquarist. For example, it has been shown that ozone used in connection with activated carbon results in the removal of a greater percentage of D.O.C. that either ozone or activated carbon alone.

This is probably because the oxidation of certain compounds by ozone renders them more likely to be adsorbed by the carbon. In much the same manner, ozone enhances the effectiveness of a protein skimmer, making organic compounds more likely to form foam.

Compounds that are resistant to breakdown by bacteria may also be rendered more amenable to such breakdown by the action of ozone.

Regardless of the mode of action, it is demonstrable that aquariums in which ozone is used are far less likely to suffer from undesirable blooms of microalgae, and that tanks already infested with microalgae can be rid of these pests by adding an ozonizer.

The lessening of the concentration of D.O.C. by ozone or any other means also has beneficial effects for fishes and invertebrates, since they are not accustomed to high levels of D.O.C. in nature.

Ozone may be introduced into the aquarium via the protein skimmer, simply by placing an ozone generator in line with the air pump.

If you do this, direct the outflow of water from the skimmer (not from the waste cup) over activated carbon before returning it to the tank.

The carbon will remove any residual ozone present in the water, and, as noted above, will remove additional organic matter that has been partially oxidized by the ozone.

You can also install a special ozone reaction chamber on the tank. This device is simply an enclosed column through which water passes over a medium, such as plastic balls or pieces of ceramic, which serve to slow the water down.

Ozone is injected into this chamber, developing a slight positive pressure, which increases the solubility of ozone in the water.

All materials in contact with ozone gas must be ozone resistant, ideally of Norprene, PVC, or Teflon. If you use ordinary polyethylene air tubing for ozone, you will find that it rapidly breaks down, and leaks will develop.

Take precautions not to allow ozone to escape into the atmosphere. Although ozone generators for home aquarium use are unlikely to produce enough ozone to cause harm, even if their full output were vented into the room, ozone can cause dizziness and nausea if inhaled in sufficient quantity, and in high concentrations can be harmful to the respiratory tract.

How much ozone is needed? This will depend upon a host of factors that, unfortunately, will be different for every reef tank set-up. You want an amount of ozone sufficient to oxidize the D.O.C. present, but not an excess, which can be harmful to invertebrates.

Since the amount of D.O.C. varies according to such variables as how recently the prefilter pads were cleaned and how much and what kind of food was added today, etc., it is impossible to predict how much ozone will be required.

You can achieve the maximum benefit from ozonization if you use a redox potential controller to regulate the amount of ozone that is introduced.

Redox potential is a complicated chemical concept that represents the net result of all the oxidation-reduction reactions that are occurring in the aquarium at a given moment.

You can think of redox potential in the following way:

• Any two dissimilar metals placed into an electrolyte (a solution of chemical salts) creates a battery. (If you are inclined toward experimentation, you can demonstrate this phenomenon easily by taking a piece of copper wire and a piece of iron wire and sticking them into a potato. The juices of the potato are an electrolyte.

With a galvanometer you will be able to measure a weak electric current across the two pieces of wire in the potato.

A simple galvanometer can be made by winding several turns of wire around pocket compass. When electrical current is passed through the wire, the compass needle will move in response to the magnetic field generated.)

The seawater in an aquarium is, of course, an electrolyte. You can do the potato experiment outlined above using tank water instead of the potato, and the experiment will still work.

If, instead of the copper and iron wires used in the experiment, an electrode made of platinum and silver chloride is immersed in the tank, the measured voltage is, by definition, the redox potential of the water in the tank.

A redox meter, therefore, is simply a millivolt meter connected to a special redox electrode. A redox controller is a redox meter with electronic circuitry that permits the ozonizer to be turned on or off, to maintain the redox potential of the tank at some predetermined value which has been programmed into the device.

By analogy, a redox controller operates the ozonizer to maintain the desired redox potential in the same way that a thermostat controls the aquarium heater to maintain the desired temperature.

Of what significance is the redox potential of the aquarium?

Redox potential can be either a positive or a negative number. Readings that are positive indicate conditions more conducive to oxidation, while negative readings indicate conditions more conducive to reduction.

Many biological processes, the conversion of ammonia to nitrate, for example, or the utilization of food to provide energy, occur most readily under conditions that are conducive to oxidation. In simple terms, the redox potential of the aquarium is a measure of the ability of the system to eliminate wastes.

The higher the reading (up to a certain point, of course), the better.

What should be the redox potential of a reef tank? Let us once again observe a natural coral reef for the answer.

If redox potential of the water around a coral reef is measured, a reading of somewhere around +350 millivolts is usually obtained.

You tank should therefore be at this redox potential, or higher, up to about 450 millivolts.

A redox potential greater than 350 millivolts is often recommended on the assumption that, in the confines of an aquarium, levels of pollution that occur when food, for example, is introduced will be much higher than would ever occur in the ocean.

At a higher redox potential, the system will recover more quickly from periodic additions of food, and will thus be more stable.

To those readers unfamiliar with chemistry, I apologize for the long discussion of oxidation reductions reactions, but I think that it is important to understand these principles in order to appreciate how a piece of "high-tech" equipment like a redox controller can benefit your tank.

And to those readers who are chemists, I apologize for the oversimplification of a very complex concept.

To summarize, undesirable microalgae growth in the reef tank can be controlled by :

1) using live rock, rather than dead materials, for tank decor,

2) adding herbivorous organisms to the tank,

3) taking all possible measures to keep nitrates and phosphates to a minimum, and

4) using an ozonizer, preferably controlled by a redox controller, to maintain a redox potential of 350-450 millivolts.

✔ Water Handling.

Ask any aquarist what he or she likes least about the hobby and chances are they will say "Carrying heavy buckets of water around." With all of the pumps, filters, valves, pipes and other paraphernalia associated with reef tanks, I often find myself wishing I had studied to be a plumber, instead of a biologist.

With practice, however, I have become handy at working with PVC pipe. Once you get the hang of working with PVC, it is amazing how versatile it is.

In case it has not yet occurred to you, a few extra plumbing parts can be used to rig the system so you can drain and refill the tank with the help of the system's pump.

Here's how to do it.

Install a cutoff valve (V-1, see below), followed by a tee, between the sump outlet and the intake of the pump.

On the discharge side of the pump, install a tee and another cutoff valve (V-2), between the backflow check valve in the line between the pump and the tank, and the tank.

Note that this arrangement will not work if you do not have a check valve in the location shown in Figure 6-1.

If you do not have such a check valve in place, install one now. At around $30, check valves are much more economical than new carpeting for the den, which will cer-

FIGURE 6-1

DRAIN/FILL VALVE INSTALLATION

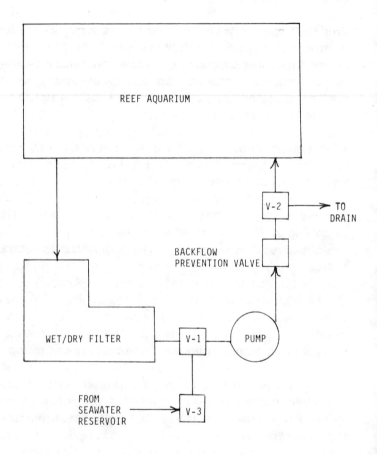

ainly be ruined if the power goes out and the tank back siphons through the pump and onto the floor while you're away for the weekend.) Install a third valve (V-3), on the side arm of he tee on the intake side of the pump.

From V-2, connect a pipe or hose (or make provisions for such a connection) leading to a convenient household drain. Note that V-2 should be located below the bottom of the tank, since we want water to siphon out of the tank through V-2 to the drain when V-2 is opened.

From V-3, provide for a connection to a pipe or hose that will be run to the container you use for mixing seawater for water changes.

See Figure 6-1 for a schematic diagram of this arrangement of valves.

I use a large plastic picnic cooler for mixing seawater. The cooler had a drain molded into one end which I removed with a hole saw, leaving a hole large enough to install a bulkhead fitting. This bulkhead fitting is connected via a hose that can be connected to V-3.

When I want to change some water, I do the following.

1. On the day before the water change, I hook up the hose from the cooler to V-3. Then I fill the cooler with purified (by reverse osmosis) freshwater at the same temperature as the tank, and add the appropriate amount of salt mix. I drop in an airstone to circulate the water in the cooler and help the salt dissolve.

2. The next day, when I am ready to change water, I first turn off the pump. Then I close both V-1 and V-3, connect the line that runs to the drain from V-2, and open V-2. When V-2 is open, water will flow from the tank to the

drain until V-2 is closed. The check valve will prevent water from flowing backwards through the pump.

3. When enough water has drained from the tank, I then close V-2, and open V-3. (At this point, always check to make doubly sure V-1 is closed.) When the pump is again turned on, it will pump water from the seawater reservoir into the tank.

4. When the tank is full again, shut off the pump. Then close V-3, open V-1, and restart the pump. You should be back to normal operation of the system.

Study Figure 6-1 and you should see that this simple arrangement will make changing water much easier.

Another water handling chore, one that I find even more aggravating that doing water changes, is adding fresh-water to compensate for evaporation.

Reef tanks lose a lot of water in this way, and topping up can be an almost daily task. It can be very convenient to install an automatic top-up system.

Here is how to do it.

You will need the following equipment: a plastic reser-voir tank of two to five gallons capacity, a peristaltic pump, and a float switch.

The best choice for a reservoir is a tank called an "aspirator carboy", which is basically a large plastic jug with a hose nipple molded into one side near the bottom.

Dealers who stock advanced equipment should have this item, or check with a scientific supply house.

The peristaltic pump is the heart of the system. This is

a type of pump used in medical and industrial applications where a slow delivery rate and no contact between pump parts and the liquid being pumped are the requirement. A good one will cost $200 to $300.

The float switch is installed in the sump of the trickle filter, and adjusted so that it will energize the peristaltic pump when the water level in the sump drops a bit due to evaporation.

You will have to experiment to determine the exact level. Make sure the float switch

1) is safe for saltwater use, and
2) has electrical specifications that match those of the pump.

You will also need enough flexible hose, and perhaps a few fittings, to connect the reservoir to the pump, and to run from the pump to the sump of the trickle filter. When the system is hooked up properly, fill the reservoir with purified fresh water.

It operates as follows: When the water level in the sump drops, the float switch closes and turns on the peristaltic pump. The pump moves freshwater from the reservoir to the sump, restoring the original level. This causes the float switch to open again, shutting off the pump.

By adjusting both the float switch and the speed of the pump (most peristaltic pumps have a speed control), you can automatically add freshwater to the system when even a small amount evaporates.

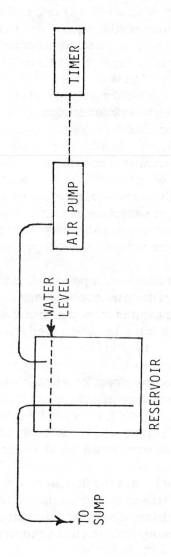

FIGURE 6-2

AUTOMATIC TOP-UP SYSTEM USING AIR PUMP AND TIMER

✔ Water Quality Maintenance.

A set-up very similar to the one just described can be employed to automatically add foods, calcium or iron supplements and similar additives to the tank automatically.

In this case the peristaltic pump is controlled not by a float switch but by a timer. By regulating the timer, measured doses of additives can be added according to a predetermined schedule.

Some additives can even be incorporated into the water in the reservoir of the evaporation top-off system, so that the system can do double duty. This takes some thought and experimentation to work properly, however.

If you cannot afford a peristaltic pump for either of the two applications mentioned above, you can accomplish almost the same result with the contraption diagrammed in Figure 6-2.

This set-up employs an airtight vessel as the reservoir. This can be anything, an empty Coke bottle with a cork in the top or an elaborate custom made plastic tank.

A length of rigid airline reaching to the bottom of the reservoir is connected to a length of flexible airline running to the sump of the trickle filter.

A second piece of rigid airline enters the top of the reservoir, but projects only into the air space above the level of liquid. This is connected to an air pump, which is controlled by a timer.

Each time the air pump is turned on, air pressure forces the liquid out of the reservoir and into the sump. Some experimentation and calculations will be required to determine the proper timer settings to dispense the appropriate amount of supplement.

Here is an example to show you how to do this.

First, set up the system with plain tap water. Run the output line from the reservoir to a container that is graduated in fluid ounces. Turn on the air pump and let it run for one minute. Make a note of the amount of liquid that has been pumped into the measuring container.

Let's say this amount is one ounce. If the entire reservoir contains one gallon of water (128 ounces), then running the air pump for one minute every day will dispense one ounce of material into the aquarium daily for 128 days.

Now it is necessary to calculate how much food, supplements or whatever to put into the reservoir. Let's say you want to add 25 drops of trace elements to the tank every day.

Since you have a 128 day supply available in the reservoir, you would add 3200 drops (32 teaspoons) of trace elements to the reservoir, and then fill it up to the one gallon mark with purified water.

Setting the timer to run the air pump for one minute every day will then automatically dispense trace elements into the tank.

Many supplements and additives can be mixed together (check with the manufacturer for specific recommendations).

Suppose in the previous example you want to add a daily dose of a calcium supplement along with the trace elements. The label says to add 10 drops per day. You would add 1280 drops (call it 13 teaspoons) of calcium

supplement along with the 32 teaspoons of trace elements, and then fill the reservoir to the one gallon mark
with water. With a little arithmetic, you can figure out
how to properly dose a variety of additives with this
same arrangement.

Using automated equipment such as redox controllers
and dosing pumps will not directly improve the conditions in your tank.

The greater stability that can be achieved through the
use of such automated devices will, however, result in
subtle, but noticeable, improvements in the health of
your invertebrates and fishes.

The main beneficiary of automated systems, though, is
you, the aquarist.

Time that was once spent in topping-off, adding supplements, or fiddling with the ozonizer can instead be spent
enjoying the tank.

Chapter Seven

Creating the Reef Environment

By now you should have a well established reef tank containing live rock.

If your water conditions are as indicated in Chapter Five, your tank should be perfect for any of the organisms found on or around coral reefs.

And, no doubt, you are anxious to add some of these beautiful creatures.

So, it's time to break out the old checkbook or credit card and head for the nearest dealer, right ?

Wrong!

Before you begin stocking up on reef organisms you should do some very careful planning, and a bit of research. Why ?

Because the fish, invertebrates and macroalgae you will find in your dealer's tanks come from a wide variety of loacations and habitats in nature.

In the small confines of a reef aquarium, even a very large one, you can hope to reproduce only a tiny segment of a real reef.

Thus, you should concentrate upon one particular type of habitat (or microenvironment, as the ecologists say), and attempt to replicate this habitat as faithfully as possible.

There is really nothing new in this approach; serious freshwater hobbyists have been keeping species tanks and habitat tanks for many many years.

All the marine hobbyist needs, in order to emulate these tried and true methods, is information.

And that is what I hope to provide.

In this chapter, we will examine some of the basic types of marine habitats you may wish to consider, and discuss in general terms how to go about creating such environments in the aquarium.

In later chapters we will look at some specific examples of reef habitats, and the types of organisms that populate them.

There are a number of advantages to combining animals from similar habitats in the same aquarium. One is that required conditions of lighting, current, etc. (i.e., anything apart from water quality itself) will be identical for organisms that live together in nature.

This makes it possible to create an optimum setting for a community of organisms, rather than settling for an average set of conditions that diverse organisms all will tolerate, but which are not really ideal for any one species.

To illustrate what I mean, consider this analogy from the realm of home gardening:

Ferns prefer a damp, shady location and a moisture retentive soil high in organic matter; cacti prefer drier, sunnier conditions, and need a well drained, preferably sandy, soil.

Now most gardeners know that certain ferns will tolerate sunny conditions, and some cacti will survive in partial shade. We can thus plant a mixed bed, containing both ferns and cacti; however, notice the verbs I used in the previous sentence: "tolerate" and "survive."

In a mixed planting of ferns and cacti, neither one will really flourish. Furthermore, the gardener who attempts such a plant combination can expect to spend a lot of time tending the planting bed.

Water the ferns, but not too well, lest the cacti drown. Fertilize the cacti, but not too much; don't want to burn the foliage on the ferns.

And on, and on; a lot of hassles, too much work, and less than perfect results, despite the effort.

If this gardening scenario reminds you too much of your marine aquarium keeping experiences to date, you can probably benefit greatly from an application of the principles I shall discuss below.

There are several basic themes one can select when creating a plan for the reef tank environment.

Each theme relates to some aspect of reef ecology. Here are some examples:

1. Geographic location (This is perhaps too broad a category, but is a basic starting point for any set-up.)

2. Water depth.

3. Reef zonation. (See Chapter 8.)

4. Community relationships. (My personal favorite.)

5. Species tanks. (One of the easiest to pull off.)

■ Geographic Location.

It is not really a good idea to mix species of fishes from the Atlantic Ocean with species from the Pacific.

One major reason is that fishes from one ocean have had no opportunity to develop a natural immunity to parasites and bacteria that are harbored by fishes from another part of the world.

The same is true for invertebrates.

One may also be surprised by unusual behavioral interactions between fish species that would not normally encounter each other on the reef. If you are unsure as to the ocean from which a particular species originates, look it up.

There are many excellent field guides and picture books available that will aid you greatly in distinguishing species from Florida, Hawaii, the Sea of Cortez, Australia, etc.

Any dealer worth his salt should be able to provide locality information about the specimens he stocks.

When considering a set-up from a particular locality, remember that some species are available only from certain parts of the world, although they may occur elsewhere.

A few species, such as the Scarlet Cleaner Shrimp (*Lysmata grabhami*), for example, are found on coral reefs throughout the world.

Don't set your sights on a Florida or Hawaii tank, however, and expect to put true stony corals in it. All corals found in U.S. waters are protected by Federal law, and any specimens you may see were illegally collected.

The same holds true for Australia.

One excellent source of information about the sources of aquarium invertebrates is "*The Manual of Marine Invertebrates*" by Martyn Haywood and Sue Wells, which should be on your bookshelf if you are keeping a reef aquarium.

■ **Water Depth**.

Assuming you have settled upon a particular geographic locality, you should next limit yourself to specific habitat types within that region.

We will discuss more specifically the various life zones associated with coral reefs in Chapter 8, but for now, let's consider one very important aspect of reef ecology: water depth.

Water depth greatly affects the distribution of many types of organisms, largely because of its influence on both intensity and spectral quality of the sunlight that reaches them. Light intensity decreases with depth.

Spectral quality changes from broad to narrow, also, with increasing depth, resulting in predominantly blue light penetrating most deeply.

Clearly, then, your lighting system requirements will be different for a tank of shallow water organisms, as opposed to deep water species.

Aquarium specimens are collected from depths ranging from a few inches to 60 feet or more, and it should be obvious that their light requirements will vary greatly.

Since most aquariums are 24 inches deep or less, it follows that organisms with widely varying light requirements will be difficult to satisfy within the confines of a single tank.

Much of the confusion and controversy surrounding the issue of aquarium lighting may simply be the result of attempts to keep a wide selection of species under one set of light conditions.

The best plan is to select species that occupy roughly similar water depths in nature, and then provide the tank with appropriate lighting.

Determining the depth from which a particular specimen was collected may be a challenge, since collectors rarely supply such data.

However, many field guides provide a depth range for the specimens they describe, and picture books that depict reef communities may note the depth at which the photograph was made.

Such books often provide excellent photos of whole communities of organisms, and thus can give you valuable ideas about how natural reefs actually look.

This can be a great help, not only in selecting specimens, but also as a guide to arranging your reef tank decor.

One excellent picture book of this type is "*The Underwater Wilderness*" by Carl Roessler, which, unfortunately, is out of print. It may be available from your local library, or through used book dealers.

Locate a copy, if you can. (Sorry, my copy is not for sale.)

■ Reef Zonation.

Within any coral reef habitat there are specific zones where particular organisms are most abundant.

Bearing in mind that you can duplicate only a small area of reef, you should necessarily concentrate on a particular zone.

We will cover reef zonation in more detail in Chapter Eight.

■ Community Relationships.

Certain species of organisms are frequently, or in some cases exclusively, found with other species of organisms.

The relationship between clownfish and anemones is a familiar example of what biologists call "symbiosis", which means living together. Fascinating examples of symbiosis exist in every reef habitat.

Often, the two symbiotic partners cannot survive without each other. A tank devoted to keeping specific partners together can be most rewarding.

■ Species Tanks.

Devoting an entire reef tank to a single species may seem a bit extravagant, but if you want to achieve a breathtaking effect, it is an aproach well worth considering.

Many kinds of corals form huge stands of just one species. All other corals are excluded, either because of water conditions, or because of successful competition on the part of the dominant coral type.

Similarly, many species of fishes live in shoals or schools, consisting of many individuals of the same species.

A spectacular Indo-Pacific species tank could be created with multiple specimens of the Flowerpot Coral (*Goniopora lobata*) and a shoal of Green Chromis (*Chromis viridis*).

Such a display would not only be beautiful, it would be easy to maintain.

To summarize, plan your reef tank to include species that live in the same area of the world, and at the same, or roughly the same, water depth.

Choose organisms from a particular zone, or that have specific symbiotic relationships, and combine these in the tank.

For maximum visual impact, devote a tank to only one or a few species of reef organisms. By attempting to duplicate a specific reef community, rather than a hodgepodge of unrelated organisms, you can achieve a reef tank that is not only beautiful but also free of many common problems.

Chapter Eight

Reef Habitats of the Florida Keys

In Chapter Seven, I covered two major factors that determine the character of coral reef faunas, geographic
location and water depth.

As an introduction to the concept of reef zonation and
ecology, let us more closely examine the various zones
and microhabitats that comprise the reef system of the
Florida Keys.

While not the most spectacular of the world's reefs, the
reef system of the Keys is one of the best studied.
Hence, much information about this area and its fauna
is available from books.

This is also the area with which I am personally best
acquainted.

Bear in mind that the area we are discussing includes
several hundred square miles, from Miami to Key West,
with some 6000 patch reefs in Hawk's Channel alone.

Water depth ranges from 0 to over 100 feet. Within the
region are numerous scattered areas of bedrock, rubble,

sand, mud and silt; turtle grass may cover acres, and abruptly give way to hard bottom areas dominated by gorgonians and scattered coral outgrowths.

In short, the area is extremely complex, and any attempt to create a generalized depiction of the patterns of life within it can at best be an approximation.

Nevertheless, zonation can be observed, and particular communities of animals and plants are associated with each zone.

Even a very large aquarium is tiny in comparison to the vastness of the offshore shallows of the Keys. Consider, for example, that about 150 pounds of live rock are required to suitably stock a 100 gallon reef tank; compare this to the 123 billion pounds of rock (that's 123,000,000,000) that, according to one recent estimate, can be found between Miami and Key West.

Clearly, one can only hope to recreate a relatively microscopic portion of this habitat in the living room or den.

As you become more familiar with the ecology of coral reefs and their environs, you will soon discover that specialization is the rule, not the exception, to the lifestyles of the organisms found there.

As aquarists, we should take our cue from Mother Nature, and create aquariums that are somewhat specialized, as well.

Let us begin our discussion of reef zonation by carefully examining the diagram presented as Figure 8-1.

This is a schematic representation of a "typical" barrier or fringing reef. The line at the top of the diagram represents the surface of the ocean.

The shore is on the left side of the diagram, the open sea, on the right.

The scale of this drawing is exaggerated, since the lagoon zone may be as much as five miles wide in some areas. Breakers form whitecaps at the reef crest, while the shallower back reef and lagoon, protected by the reef from the force of the open sea, are relatively calm.

Even in these protected areas, however, tidal surge, currents and wind driven wave action create constant water movement.

In areas where turtle grass grows, water movement is reduced by the thick carpet of plants.

As a result, suspended particles are deposited among the grass blades, and the silt may be several feet deep.

Turtle grass beds thus act as giant filters, efficiently removing nutrient laden debris that washes outward from the shore.

Where rocky outcrops occur within the lagoon zone, patch reefs may form when the rocks are colonized by corals and other organisms from the main reef nearby.

When patch reefs are distantly isolated from other, similar underwater "structure," they may harbor a surprisingly diverse assemblage of fishes.

This feature makes some patch reefs quite popular with divers, since many species can be found within a relatively small area.

Seaward of the lagoon zone lies the reef itself, which may be subdivided into four major life zones: the rear zone, the reef crest, the mixed zone, and the fore reef.

FIGURE 8-1

TYPICAL REEF ZONATION IN THE FLORIDA KEYS

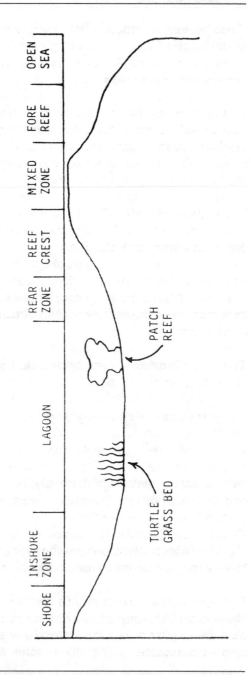

Each zone has its own characteristics and its own community of species, although many reef organisms, certain shrimps and fishes, for example, may occur in several different areas.

The rear zone, like the lagoon lying shoreward of it, is protected by the reef from the pounding of the open sea. Here are found many species of shallow water corals, soft corals, calcareous algae, and many organisms from the lagoon.

Sea mats may be locally abundant in the rear zone, so much so that reef ecologists often designate a "*Zoanthus* zone" to emphasize this fact.

The reef crest, scoured by the breaking surf, is usually dominated by branching staghorn and elkhorn corals that require sediment free water, bright light and abundant oxygen.

These corals grow so rapidly that they completely dominate the reef crest. Few aquarium specimens are collected from these turbulent, dangerous waters, although many species of fish seek shelter among the branching corals.

Seaward of the reef crest, as the reef begins to slope outward and downward to the abyss of the open ocean, one finds the richest diversity of species.

Water depth over the mixed zone and the fore reef zone plays a major role in determining what types of invertebrates may be found in these areas.

Ecologists often further subdivide these zones, to reflect the special characteristics of communities of organisms that develop at a particular depth, or over a particular type of substrate.

It is readily apparent from the foregoing discussion, which, incidentally, is a greatly simplified explanation of reef zonation, that a great variety of specialized habitats occurs both on and around the coral reef.

Note also that the pattern of zonation described above may be repeated to some degree among the diverse reef habitats of the Indo-Pacific.

No natural reef, even in the Keys, will exactly fit this pattern, however. There are always variations, depending upon local conditions.

Nevertheless, a particular habitat usually will predictably contain certain species of invertebrates, and these constitute the community of species you would want to select for a reef tank reflecting a particular zone.

Let's start back at the inshore zone again, and consider the types of organisms that may be found there. I will restrict this discussion to organisms that are available in the aquarium trade, since many easily kept aquarium species are found in the inshore zone.

Since rubble rock and outcrops sometimes occur in the inshore zone, occasional strays from deeper water may also be found.

One of my favorite spots in the Keys is a huge, bowl-shaped tide pool just off U.S. 1. Protected from wave action by a seawall of coral rock rubble, this pool is a giant natural aquarium.

Dozens of species of macroalgae, including *Caulerpa prolifera*, *C. racemosa*, *C. sertularoides*, *C. mexicana*, *Chondrus*, *Chaetomorpha*, *Valonia*, *Acetabularia*, *Halimeda*, *Dasycladus*, *Cymopolia*, and *Penicillus* all occur here, just to name some of the more easily identified species. On the shady side of large boulders may be found colorful sponges, including *Chondrilla*, the chicken liver sponge, which can be kept successfully in the reef tank.

Scattered among the rubble and pebbles, the lovely giant fanworm, *Sabellastarte magnifica* extends its feathery fan, feeding on plankton. These worms prefer quiet, sheltered locations and are common in boat slips and on submerged pilings.

Other species of fanworms, though none as large as *Sabellastarte*, are commonly found in such areas, as well.

Rock or flower anemones (*Phymanthus crucifer*) live in crevices between the cobbles, often in only a few inches of water.

When the rocks are exposed at low tide, or when the anemone is disturbed by inquisitive fingers, it retracts completely beneath the substrate.

Another anemone that retracts into a crevice when disturbed is the Curleycue Anemone (*Bartholomea annulata*). This anemone may be identified by the pale bands that spiral around each tentacle.

The bands contain stinging cells with which the anemone catches prey, although because of its symbiotic algae the anemone does not need to rely on catching plankton for food.

Several species of shrimps may often be found in association with the Curleycue Anemone, and an interesting marine tank could be set up featuring this community of species alone. In a burrow at the base of the anemone live pairs of Curleycue Shrimp (*Alpheus armatus*), often sold as "red pistol shrimp." Males can be distinguished from females by the striped antennae of the former.

Each pair of shrimp stakes out a particular anemone as home turf, and will vigorously defend this position against any intruder, even fish much larger than the shrimp. (For this reason, only one pair of Curleycue Shrimp can be kept together in the aquarium, as males will fight until one is dismembered.)

When the anemone is approached by a fish or diver, the shrimp marches boldly from its burrow and emits a loud "pop!" using one of its claws, which is specialized for this purpose.

The sound is audible from a considerable distance, and is apparently enough to frighten away fishes that would otherwise feed on the anemone.

In this fashion, the anemone is protected by the shrimp. The shrimp, in turn, receives protection from shrimp-eating fishes, owing to the stinging tentacles of the anemone.

Other shrimps, such as Pederson's Cleaning Shrimp (*Periclimenes pedersoni*), Sexy Shrimp (*Thor amboinensis*), and Spotted Cleaning Shrimp (*Periclimenes yucatanensis*), seek shelter among the tentacles of the Curleycue Anemone.

The long, white antennae of the cleaner shrimps, together with their distinctive swaying movements, advertise their services to fishes seeking removal of parasites and dead tissue.

Fish approach the shrimp's "cleaning station," and indicate their desire to be cleaned by adopting special postures or color patterns.

The shrimp will then leave the protective tentacles of the anemone and alight on the fish's body, moving about, even inside the mouth and gill covers, extracting parasites, dead tissue and loose scales.

These the shrimp eats, so both fish and shrimp derive benefit from the cleaning relationship.

Throughout the inshore zone, among rubble, under rocks and in crevices, brittlestars abound. While not particularly popular with aquarists, owing to their secretive habits, brittlestars make a fine addition to the aquarium.

Many species sport attractive colors and patterns, and all are excellent scavengers, coming out at night to feed on bacteria, plankton, debris or bits of dead animal matter. One species, the Reticulated Brittle Star (*Ophionereis reticulata*), is especially abundant among beds of the calcareous alga *Halimeda*.

This brittlestar has a unique way of defending itself against predators when it leaves the safety of the *Halimeda* to forage at night. When disturbed, its entire body flashes with a brilliant yellow green light (bioluminescence).

This reaction presumably dazzles the would-be predator, allowing the brittlestar sufficient time to escape.

Brittlestars are so called because they are easily damaged by handling, and will not survive in the aquarium if they are not provided with shelter into which they can retire to escape the light. Bear this in mind if you decide to obtain a specimen.

Major areas of the inshore zone of the Florida Keys are occupied by beds of Turtle Grass (*Thalassia*), which can be grown in the aquarium if you provide a thick substrate of fine silt.

Since this is not easy to do with conventional reef system filtration, aquarists who wish to duplicate the Turtle Grass habitat may resort to plastic copies of Vallisneria, sold for freshwater tanks.

The nutrient rich substrate of the grass beds is home to literally hundreds of species of seaweeds, all those mentioned earlier, plus many more.

Here also one finds the Florida Pink-Tipped Anemone (*Condylactis passiflora*) in abundance, the amusing Carrier Urchin (*Lytechinus variegatus*), so named because of its habit of carrying objects as camouflage, and the Giant Seahorse (*Hippocampus* erectus).

Larval and juvenile fishes occur in abundance in the grass beds, where they find both food and shelter among the fronds. Here also one finds damselfishes, several types of wrasse, and the Southern Stingray.

Reticulated sea stars, the "Bahama Star" of the aquarium trade (*Oreaster reticulata*) and the Five Toothed Sea Cucumber (*Actinopyga agassizi*, which, by the way, has its teeth in its anus rather than its mouth) are large, conspicuous inhabitants.

The Five Toothed Sea Cucumber is sometimes host to the Pearlfish (*Carapus bermudensis*), which lives inside the cucumber's digestive tract, emerging only at night to feed.

Long-Spined Sea Urchins (*Diadema antillarum*) may also be found in Turtle Grass beds, and the Queen Conch (*Strombus gigas*) was once common here.

Queen conchs have been over-harvested for food and their lovely pink shells, and are now protected. Fortunately, this mollusk is now available to aquarists from a hatchery in the Cayman Islands, and makes an excellent algae scavenger.

Several small coral species are found in grass beds, and all, according to researchers, can be kept successfully in the aquarium.

None of these would be available to hobbyists, however, since all corals in American waters are protected.

The open waters of the lagoon may be dotted with tiny patch reefs, and here an abundance of organisms more commonly seen on the reef proper may be found.

Curleycue and Pink-Tipped Anemones may be seen, along with the Giant Caribbean Anemone (*Condylactis gigantea*), called "Haitian Pink-Tip Anemone" in the aquarium trade.

The Stinging, or Antler, Anemone (*Lebrunia danae*) occurs here and there in the lagoon, along with the pretty blue-green Neon Disc Anemone (*Paradiscosoma elegans*).

Several other small anemones are found in the lagoon zone, and these may turn up from time to time in Florida shipments.

In areas of the lagoon where hard bottom or rubble occurs, different animals can be found. Hard bottom lagoons often become forests of gorgonians.

These beautiful soft corals have an associated fauna consisting of many suitable reef tank species.

At the time of this writing, the question of whether to prohibit collection of gorgonians in Florida is an open one. We will assume, for purposes of this discussion, that you will be able to buy Florida gorgonians.

All of the lagoon species make good aquarium specimens, provided they are properly collected still attached to a chunk of rock.

Their names are descriptive of their appearance: Deadman's Fingers, Knobby Candelabrum, Sea Rod, Common Bushy Soft Coral, Smooth Sea Feather, and Yellow Sea Blade, to name a few.

Colorful sponges, seaweeds, fragile-looking tunicates in yellow, blue and orange, anemones large and small, and a variety of crustaceans, can be found in these gorgonian "forests."

Indeed, an impressive reef tank could be created to feature only the animals of this habitat.

Sandy or muddy bottoms with rubble are most likely to be found carpeted with the Green Sea Mat (*Zoanthus sociatus*). This colorful and popular aquarium species is at home in any tank with sufficiently bright light.

I have seen sea mat colonies completely exposed at low tide, baking under the tropical sun at temperatures in excess of 100 degrees F.

No wonder this species is hardy in the aquarium!

Chapter Nine

Deep Reefs and Caves

In Chapter Eight, I discussed reef habitats in the lagoon region between the shore and the reef itself. As one approaches the back reef zone from offshore, the bottom usually slopes upward to the reef crest.

Turbulence characterizes the reef crest, and few animals are collected here because this region is dangerous to a swimmer.

Cross the reef crest to the seaward side, the fore reef, and you will find the greatest abundance and diversity of life. Many of the species of true reef animals that are seen in dealers' tanks are collected from the fore reef zone.

As one moves away from the reef crest across the fore reef and toward the open ocean, the bottom slopes down, down, down, until it merges with the dark, cold depths of the abyss.

Most of the invertebrates I will discuss in this chapter can be found somewhere on the fore reef, but they all share one special quality that makes them of particular interest. They don't need light. If you are dismayed by the cost of a good quality lighting system for your reef tank, I offer an alternative plan.

All of the species I will cover in this chapter come from deep water, or live in caves, or simply have no special lighting needs.

Thus, while good water quality is a must for these species, you need to provide only enough light to see and appreciate their beauty. And most of them are very beautiful, indeed.

Representatives of every major group are included among the deep water and cave fauna. I will discuss each group in turn below.

We will omit a discussion of crustaceans (shrimps, crabs, etc.), none of which require light, but, by all means include specimens of crustaceans in your tank, if you wish.

Caves are special habitats that mimic the cool, dark waters of the deep reef. Indeed, many organisms commonly found in deep water are found in caves located in shallower depths. Thus, cave dwellers will also be at home in a deep reef tank.

Keep the temperature of your deep reef/cave tank at 75 degrees, and provide the same water conditions that you would for any other reef aquarium (See Chapter Five).

Remember that organisms that do not contain symbiotic algae, the one's we are concerned with here, depend upon plankton and detritus for food. Therefore, a deep reef tank will require feeding.

I get excellent results with Coralife Gourmet Gumbo, Coralife Target Food, and Florida Aqua Farms Roti Rich as well as Coral Nutrient from Thiel Aqua Tech.

I supplement these foods with live baby brine shrimp. Frozen baby brine shrimp and frozen plankton are also satisfactory.

Remember that when it comes to feeding any reef tank "less is more."

Feed very sparingly, especially for the first month or two, and evaluate the health, growth and general appearance of your specimens before increasing the amount of food.

Monitor water quality frequently, using good test kits, and carry out frequent, small partial water changes.

Good current is important for plankton feeding organisms, also. Provide additional currents by installing powerheads in the tank.

Hair algae growth is generally not a problem in a dimly illuminated tank, but an effort should be made to keep nitrates and phosphates to a minimum, lest you encourage the very unsightly and undesirable red, black and blue-green slime algae.

Phosphates and nitrates can be controlled as described in Chapter Five.

Following is a listing of organisms that are suitable for a deep reef or cave tank.

This is not an exhaustive listing, but most of the organisms I will mention are readily available.

• Coelenterates.

While most coelenterates require very bright illumination, several types prefer shade or darkness.

Among anemones, the tube-dwelling species have no symbiotic algae, and do very well in a deep reef tank. Tube anemones have two sets of tentacles. The outer rows are quite long, and the inner ones, surrounding the mouth, are much shorter.

A species commonly imported from the Indian Ocean is a beautiful orange-pink color, and can extend to 10 inches across the crown of tentacles.

Purple and brown colored tube anemones are often available, and are usually collected in the Caribbean.

All tube anemones live buried in substrate, lining the burrow with a tube made of a mucus secretion. When freshly collected, the tube is usually heavily encrusted with mud. This should have been removed by the dealer before placing the anemone on display, as the mud can easily foul a tank.

If this is not the case, however, gently and carefully remove the anemone from the tube, and place it in the tank. It will soon construct a new tube, and bury itself in the substrate.

If you do not have a layer of substrate on the bottom of the tank (and this is to be avoided with reef tanks), you can create an area for a tube anemone by placing a circle of rocks on the bottom, much like outlining a flower bed, and fill the center with sand.

Only one species of tube anemone should be kept in the tank, as the different species can sting each other. Be aware, also, that tube anemones can catch small fishes, including clownfish. Feed them a small piece of frozen fish, or a guppy, once a week.

Only one true coral commonly available to the aquarist is suitable for the deep reef tank. This is *Tubastrea*, the Orange Polyp Coral, as it is sometimes called. Bright orange colonies the size of a tennis ball are often collected from caves and underneath ledges in the Pacific.

Tubastrea is easy to care for. Provide a good, strong current, directed sideways across the the coral colony, not pointed straight at it.

Use a small amount of Coralife Appetite Stimulant, sprayed in the general vicinity of the coral, to encourage the coral to extend its bright yellow tentacles.

Then feed each member of the colony separately on plankton, brine shrimp, or a small piece of chopped shrimp or fish. Feeding should be done in the evenings, two or three times a week.

Aquarists who take care to treat *Tubastrea* in this way will be rewarded with the growth of new polyps over several month's time. This coral has reached six inches in diameter in careful hobbyists' tanks.

While *Tubastrea* is the only commonly available true coral that can do without light, many soft corals and gorgonians are suitable for the dimly lit reef tank.

Certainly the loveliest is the soft coral *Dendronephyta*, usually known as "Colored Flower Coral". Two species, *Dendronephyta klunzingeri* and *D. rubeola*, are frequently imported.

Both species appear to have been made from hand-blown glass, and their loosely branched, fragile-looking colonies come in shades of pink and yellow-orange.

This soft coral actually does poorly if exposed to very bright light, and is often considered delicate in the aquarium. While it can be challenging to keep, I suspect most failures are due to too infrequent feedings.

Feed *Dendronephyta* live baby brine shrimp every day, in small quantities, and it will reward you with surprisingly rapid growth, and the appearance of tiny, new colonies nearby.

It will rapidly die, however, if the temperature of the aquarium exceeds 75 degrees for any but the briefest period of time. Consider adding a chiller system to your set-up, if you plan on keeping this soft coral.

Another species, as yet unidentified, is sold under the name "Cactus Coral" or "Strawberry Coral". With its lumpy, wine colored appearance when contracted, it looks unimpressive.

When it expands in the evening, however, and displays its feathery white polyps extending from the strawberry colored body, the contrast is most attractive.

This species has proven itself to be extremely hardy in the aquarium, and tolerates abuse that would spell disaster for many species. Place it where you want it and then leave it alone, as it will attach itself to surrounding rocks rather quickly.

No special feeding is required, apart from the general guidelines already mentioned.

So many gorgonians are available for the deep reef tank that I will not attempt to catalog them by species.

Suffice it to say that gorgonians with polpys colored any color other than brown or green most likely do not require light.

Those with red, orange or yellow bodies, or with pure white polyps, certainly do not require light. All gorgonians like good current, and all do need frequent feeding, ideally with live baby brine shrimp.

Two especially good species deserve mention. The deepwater brown and white "Mexican Gorgonian" (which looks like a tumbleweed), grows surprisingly rapidly in the tank, and the "Red Finger Gorgonian" (which is sparsely branched, like a dead tree, red in color with white polyps) is amazingly hardy.

I once discovered a specimen of Red Finger Gorgonian, nearly covered with detritus, in the corner of a holding vat used for curing live rock. It had apparently been placed there by mistake and had gone unnoticed for several weeks (months?).

I removed it from the vat, and plopped it into a corner of a reef tank, where it expanded its polyps within hours, and where it continues to live today.

Inspect all gorgonians carefully for damage before purchasing. If the colored tissue is hanging loosely from the brown, woody internal skeleton, chances are an infection has set in, and the colony will die.

If, however, there are areas, especially near the base of the colony, where tissue is missing entirely but the polyps are expanded and other areas of the specimen appear in good shape, the gorgonian is probably in good health.

If the colored tissue is missing at the tips of the branches, you can safely prune off the internal skeleton just above the point where the colored tissue stops, using a pair of sterilized nail scissors.

From the above discussion, it is easy to see that a rather impressive tank could be created using deep water or cave dwelling *coelenterates* alone; however, there are other creatures suitable for such a tank.

• **Sponges**.

Most species of sponges that are collected for the aquarium do best in shady locations, as they are easily "swamped" if algae growth gets started on them.

Sponges have a porous body, and it is through the pores that they feed and acquire oxygen. If algae or detritus are allowed to accumulate, clogging the pores, the sponge will suffocate and die.

Various species of bright red and orange sponges are imported regularly, from both the Indo-Pacific and Caribbean regions, but try to locate the beautiful blue *Adocia*.

This sponge is sometimes imported from Indonesia, but is more often seen in shipments from Hawaii.

There are three basic requirements in the care of sponges.

Make certain that the sponge is never removed from the water, otherwise, air may be trapped inside, and the sponge will slowly die from within.

Second, never allow detritus or algae to accumulate on the surface of the sponge, as noted above.

Third, supply good current.

Sponges feed primarily on very small particles, and possibly absorb dissolved organic materials, such as proteins, from the water. Therefore, no special feeding is necessary.

The physiology of sponges is poorly understood, but it is known that some species extract certain trace elements from the water.

Regular partial water changes should provide sufficient trace elements, but if you are lazy about this, at least add a good quality trace element supplement every two weeks.

In my experience, sponges do well in the reef tank, if these simple requirements are met.

• **Worms**.

All of the commonly available tubeworms will thrive without any special lighting, and can thus be included in the deep reef tank.

Available species include *Sabellastarte magnifica*, which comes from Florida and the Caribbean, *S. sanctijosephi*, which comes from Hawaii, and *Spirobranchus giganteus*, which is found on reefs throughout the world.

Various other tubeworms, including *Sabella melanostigma*, *S. elegans*, *Spirographis*, *Spirobranchus tetraceros*, and many more, are either imported individually, or can be found on live rock specimens.

All are very easily kept, and need no special feeding.

Sabellastarte will toss off its crown of tentacles if dissolved oxygen levels drop much below saturation, or in response to poor water quality.

If these conditions are promptly corrected, however, the worm will regrow its "feathers" in a few months time.

Interstingly, this worm also casts off its tentacles in preparation for reproduction. If your specimen loses its tentacles and all water quality parameters are correct, you can assume that the worm is preparing to release eggs or sperm into the water.

This event may manifest itself as a milky cloud flowing from the opening of the worm's tube. Do not be alarmed, as this material will provide food for other filter feeding invertebrates in the tank.

• **Echinoderms**.

Nearly all echinoderms prefer at least a shady spot in which to retreat from time to time. This is especially true of brittle, serpent and feather stars, which are active mainly at night.

Truly deep water species of serpent star are bright red in color, and, because they are often available, can easily be included in a deep reef tank.

Brittlestars and serpent stars are not fussy eaters, although serpent stars, in particular, should occassionally be fed a small piece of fish or shrimp. Most of the time, these organisms will feed on stray bits of this and that, which they locate during their nocturnal excursions around the tank.

Feather stars, on the other hand, and the similar but distantly related basket stars, are much more fragile and difficult to keep. These specimens are not to be recommended to the beginning reef enthusiast, but are beautiful, if challenging, additions to the tank.

With some exceptions, regular starfish are to be avoided in a tank filled with sessile invertebrates, as they have the habit of eating anything and everything.

The exceptions, however, are quite desirable, and make attractive additions to the tank. These include the Blue Starfish, *Linckia laevigata*. There is also a bright purple *Linckia* available.

Two species of *Fromia*, the Red Starfish, *F. elegans*, and the Orange Starfish, *F. monilis*, also make good additions to the deep reef aquarium.

Check the *Manual of Marine Invertebrates* for photos of these species, since a mistaken identification can result in the starfish feeding on other specimens in the tank.

Sea urchins are vegetarians, and are often placed in the reef tank for algae control. This can be done in the deep reef tank, as well, but urchins are really out of place in this habitat, since they generally frequent shallower waters where their food source occurs.

All sea cucumbers can be kept in the deep reef tank. Especially attractive is the Sea Apple, *Pseudocolochirus axiologus*.

This species, along with the interesting Medusa "Worm" cucumber, *Ophiodesoma tricolor*, make good additions to any aquarium, as do any of the other colorful cucumber species that are imported.

Cucumbers are either burrowers or filter feeders. The latter are best suited to the aquarium, and can be recognized by the fact that their tentacles are feathery and highly branched, not shaped like little goblets or otherwise.

Burrowing cucumbers need silty substrate in which to burrow, since they feed like earthworms, ingesting the substrate and digesting the edible matter therein.

They are thus poor choices for the aquarium.

Bear in mind that filter-feeding cucumbers will slowly starve if not given regular feedings of plankton or plankton substitutes. The telltale sign of insufficient feeding is a reduction in the size of the animal.

• **Mollusks**.

While all mollusks with shells can be kept in the deep reef aquarium, some are better choices than others.

One that I can highly recommend is the Flame Scallop, *Lima scabra*, from Florida and the Caribbean. A related species, sometimes seen, from the Indo-Pacific is called the Flashing Flame Scallop, because waves of biolumi-nescence coruscate over its mantle in rhythmic patterns.

These two species seem to prefer dark or shady habitats. The most common reason for aquarium death of Flame Scallops is lack of food.

Under good conditions, however, they will reproduce in the tank. You will move a piece of rock one day, and discover tiny flame scallops attached to the underside.

For most other mollusks, I suggest you purchase a good sea shell identification book and learn to recognize the species which you think are attractive. Accurate identification is of utmost importance with mollusks, since their habits and diets vary widely.

I have seen harmless species displayed side by side with

predatory ones in dealer tanks, and you may take home a purchase that will delight in feeding on soft corals, for example, if you do not inform yourself of their behavior before you buy.

A host of other species of marine invertebrates live in deep water or in caves, and many of them make good aquarium inhabitants.

The species I have mentioned here should all be available from dealers who stock a wide variety of invertebrates. All of the species I have covered, in fact, could be kept together if your tank is sufficiently large. If you are interested in marine invertebrates, a deep reef tank could be a good place to start.

As I said at the beginning of this chapter, one of the nice things about choosing this habitat as a theme for your miniature reef is that you need no special lighting. Thus, you can save some money on the set-up and spend it instead on specimens, and the proper foods for them.

Chapter Ten

Invertebrates That Require Light

We have explored the habits of some of the many invertebrates that live in deep water, or in caves, or which have no special lighting requirements.

Now we shall turn our attention to the group of organisms that were the reason the reef tank craze began — the corals and their relatives.

All of these organisms are found in areas where they receive light, and all require light in order to survive and flourish in the aquarium. All are members of the ancient phylum *Coelenterata*, the *coelenterates*.

The requirement for light by tropical *coelenterates* results from the special partnership between these organisms and microscopic, single-celled algae called *zooxanthellae*.

Like all algae, *zooxanthellae* are photosynthetic, that is, they manufacture sugars from carbon dioxide and water, utilizing the energy of sunlight to carry out this chemical transformation.

A by-product of the photosynthesis reaction is pure oxygen. The evolutionary innovation that made photo-synthesis possible was the development of chlorophyll, an event that occurred over a billion years ago.

Coelenterates are very simple organisms. They consist of just two layers of tissue, forming a sac-like body with an opening at one end that serves as both mouth and anus.

The inner layer of tissue, lining the mouth opening and the internal gut cavity, consists of cells that secrete digestive juices, muscle cells that allow the animal limited movement, and reproductive cells.

The outer tissue layer contains epidermal cells, nerve cells, and specialized stinging cells. The stinging cells are commonly arrayed along fingerlike tentacles sur-rounding the mouth.

The ring of tentacles gives many coelenterates the appearance of flowers, perhaps one of the reasons for the popularity of this group with aquarists.

While some coelenterates are free-swimming forms, such as the familiar jellyfish, all of the species in which aquarists are interested bear the flower-like form, and are called polyps. There are many different kinds of polyp animals.

Polyps are generally stationary animals, attached to a solid surface by their foot, or "basal disc". Projecting upward from the basal disc is a stalk or column.

The mouth is usually centered in the top of the column, and the surrounding circle of tentacles is extended into the water, where small organisms and particles can be captured as they drift past in the currents. (The mouth and circle of tentacles are collectively called the "oral disc".) This is apparently a very successful mode of life, since polyps have been around for millions of years, and many of them still feed exclusively in this manner today.

Many variations upon this basic theme of polyp design occur. The basal disc may be broad and flat, or almost pointed. The column may be short and thick, or long and slender. The tentacles may be numerous, few, or absent entirely. Individual polyps may lead a solitary life, may occur as loose aggregations of several individuals, or may be fused together to form colonies in which all the polyps are connected by tissue.

The groups into which polyps are sorted by biologists generally include organisms that share characteristics. For example, anemones are solitary, soft corals are colonial. Incidentally, the color of the polyps, or of the colony, has little, if any, bearing upon the identification of the specimen.

At some point, (the exact time is shrouded in the ancient mists of geological history), perhaps around 600 million years ago, the partnership between polyps and *zooxanthellae* evolved.

This relationship was a great step forward, for it freed the polyp from its dependence upon food-bearing water currents, and also made possible the deposition by the polyp of a skeleton of calcium carbonate.

These two features of the polyp-zooxanthellae relationship set the stage for the development of coral reefs, and thus made possible an ecosystem wherein could develop the diversity of beautiful organisms that we enjoy in our reef tanks today.

The exact nature of the relationship between polyps

and *zooxanthellae* has yet to be fully elucidated. We know that *zooxanthellae* produce food, in the form of sugars and other carbohydrates, that is used by the polyp.

Perhaps vitamins or other important compounds are produced, as well. We know that wastes from the polyp, such as carbon dioxide and ammonia, are utilized by the *zooxanthellae*.

The exchange of food and wastes between the two symbiotic partners makes for efficient recycling of nutrients — a decided advantage in the nutrient poor waters of the coral reef.

Zooxanthellae also contribute, by means not yet fully understood, to the deposition of the calcium carbonate skeleton of true corals, making possible the actual construction of the reef itself.

Deposition of the skeleton occurs at a much faster rate in corals with *zooxanthellae* than in those without them. Clearly, the importance of this relationship to the ecology of the reef cannot be overestimated.

Even though scientists have yet to work out the details of the partnership between polyps and their *zooxanthellae*, the implication of this symbiosis for the reef aquarist is clear.

Zooxanthellae are absolutely required for the survival of the coelenterates that harbor them. Therefore, we must provide aquarium conditions conducive to the survival of the *zooxanthellae* if we expect to be able to keep the host polyp organisms alive for any length of time.

Following is a compendium of coelenterates for the reef tank. I have grouped them as they are grouped by biologists, with the scientific name of the group in parentheses after the common name.

- **Anemones (Order** *Actinaria***).**

Anemone polyps are solitary, often quite large (up to several feet across in some species). Their color is highly variable, and depends more upon the location from which the anemone was collected than upon other factors.

For aquarium purposes, the anemones may be divided into two groups: those that are suitable hosts for clownfish, and those that are not.

Clownfish host anemones include some of the most attractive species, as well as some of the largest. All are collected in the Pacific and Indian Oceans, as clownfish do not occur in the Atlantic.

Identification may be difficult in some cases, and positive identification requires microscopic examination of the tissues.

Available species include:

Heteractis magnifica, formerly known as *Radianthus ritteri*, may be called *Ritteri*, *Radianthus*, African Red Radianthus, Yellow-Tipped Long Tentacle, and various other names.

This anemone is a good host for *ocellaris*, *percula* and several other clownfish species.

The basal disc is broad and flat, and is usually attached to a solid surface, but is rarely buried in the substrate. Color of the column varies from brown to pinkish, mauve, deep red, or blue.

The numerous long tentacles are slightly inflated at the tips, and the tips are usually white or yellow in color, or at least are noticeably lighter than the rest of the tentacle.

H. magnifica needs strong light and good current, else it will wander all over the tank. Studies have indicated that in nature *H. magnifica* is most often found atop an underwater prominence. It may have a natural tendency to climb to such a location.

Duplicating this situation in the aquarium may encourage the anemone to stay put where you want it.

Heteractis aurora is also called the Mat, Aurora, or Button Anemone, and is easily recognized by hobbyists by the broad flat crown of tentacles pressed close to the substrate.

Each tentacle is transversely striped, in alternating bands of white and browninsh, and may have knobby projections along its length. The column is generally pink or yellow, and is virtually always buried in the substrate, out of sight.

Occasionally, the entire animal is yellow with pink markings. The tentacles exhibit regular, jerky movements, as if small particles were being flipped into the mouth (not actually the case). This movement adds interest to the specimen.

Four to six inch specimens are good hosts for many clownfish species. *H. aurora* was formerly called *Radianthus simplex*, under which name you may find it listed in older books.

Heteractis crispa is probably the Sebae Anemone of the aquarium trade.

The tips of the tentacles are virtually always purple or hot pink in color, with the rest of the anemone pale cream colored, white or bluish, although spectacular bright yellow and intensely pink specimens occur.

The latter color forms usually command a higher price.

Unfortunately, "counterfeit" colored Sebae Anemones appear from time to time. The anemones are dyed yellow or purple, and are sold at a premium price. They generally do not survive for more than a few weeks after the dye treatment.

To be absolutely certain that the specimen you want is not died, ask the dealer to hold it for a month before you buy. It should look as good at the end of that time as it initially did. Dyed anemones have an "artificial" look, and the coloration may not be uniform over the entire anemone.

The numerous tentacles of the Sebae Anemone are stubby, and are appressed to the substrate, with the column buried. This species, as you might guess from its common name, is a good host for Sebae clownfish. It is also accepted by Skunk, Tomato, Maroon, and *ephippium* clowns.

Another, very similar species is *Heteractis malu*, which, for aquarium purposes is identical to *H. crispa*.

Entacmaea quadricolor is usually called the Bulb, or Bubble Anemone, because the tips of the tentacles are inflated into bulbs that look like the nipple of a baby bottle.

This species comes in many shades of brown, mauve and greenish, but specimens with pinkish columns and green tentacles are the most attractive. This is an excellent host anemone for many species of clownfish. The shape of the tentacles makes identification easy. Specimens of this (or perhaps a closely related species) that are a uniform rose-pink color all over are sold as the Rose Anemone.

This color variety is rare, and specimens may cost $100 or more.

Macrodactyla doreensis is most often sold as the Long Tentacle Anemone. It is a good host for Tomato, Maroon, Sebae, Skunk, and *ephippium* clownfish, and is usually rejected by *ocellaris* and *percula* clowns.

This very commonly available species usually has a column the color of fresh salmon with white or bluish tentacles. A form with deep purple tentacles is sometimes available, and makes a striking addition to the tank. Around the column just below the tentacles are numerous small bumps or tubercles. The column is virtually always buried in the substrate.

Many coelenterates can sting or "nettle" each other. Of those above, all the *Heteractis* species can be kept together, or with *Entacmaea*, but do not keep them with *Macrodactyla*.

A notable exception is *H. crispa* (or *H. malu*) which can be kept with *Macrodactyla*, but not with other *Heteractis* species.

None of the species listed above can be kept with carpet anemones.

Stichodactyla gigantea is the Giant Carpet Anemone of the aquarium trade. This, and all other carpet anemones, can be identified by the very numerous, short tentacles that completely cover the oral disc, giving the overall appearance of a shag carpet. Most specimens are brown, but bright green, and even turquoise blue, specimens are available.

All carpet anemones are good clownfish hosts, and are particularly preferred by the Saddleback clownfish.

Stichodactyla haddoni is usually called the Saddle Carpet Anemone, because of the association between it and the Saddleback clownfish. In virtually all specimens, the tentacles are of two colors, giving an overall variegated effect to the oral disc. The margin of the oral disc of this anemone is ruffled, and does not lie flat against the substrate as in the Giant Carpet.

Stichodactyla mertensii, Merten's Carpet Anemone, is also imported for the aquarium, and is difficult to distinguish from a brown specimen of the Giant Carpet. Tentacles are fewer in number, shortere and not so closely packed as in the other two species.

Two regularly imported Indo-Pacific anemones that I have not been able to identify precisely are the "Purple Mat" anemone, and the "Dwarf" anemone.

The former resembles *H. aurora*, but with smooth tentacles that are bright purple in color, while the latter resembles *H. magnifica*. Both are small species, usually about four inches in diameter, but I do not think that these are merely small specimens of the larger anemones which they resemble.

The Hawaiian Anemone, *Antheopsis papillosa*, may also be called the "Sand" anemone. It is either white or pale pink in color, and the column is buried in the substrate.

Despite the fact that clownfish do not occur in Hawaii, this species is often "adopted" by clowns who are given no other choice. Do not keep this species with other anemones, as "nettling" can occur.

None of the Atlantic anemones are suitable hosts for clownfish, although clowns will sometimes take up residence in one of these species if there is no other anemone available.

Never keep Atlantic anemones with the Indo-Pacific species, as "nettling" will almost surely occur. (In such cases, you will most often find that the more expensive specimen is killed by the cheaper one.)

Atlantic anemones have the advantage of being much cheaper than their Indo-Pacific counterparts, and make beautiful additions to a Caribbean or Florida theme tank.

Species include:
Condylactis passiflora, the Florida Pink Tip anemone, probably the most common and widely available of all anemones. Specimens are variable in color, generally in shades of pink, cream, white or a combination of these colors. Easy to keep, these anemones are extraordinarily abundant in turtle grass beds in the Florida Keys.

Condylactis gigantea, is called the Haitian Pink Tip Anemone in the aquarium business. It differs from the more common Florida Pink Tip in that the tips of the tentacles are slightly inflated, the column is almost always pink or reddish in color, and the tentacles are greenish in color with a definite pattern of shading that is difficult to describe.

This species also grows much larger, and is found on reefs, not in turtle grass beds. The two species of *Condylactis* may be kept together in the aquarium.

Several Atlantic anemones are known as "Flower" or

"Rock" anemones, and are usually found in the inter-tidal zone. The most frequently imported of these is *Phymanthus crucifer*, a highly variable species with variegated tentacles located just at the margin of the oral disc, and with a very short, stubby column.

Other species called flower anemones may be superficially similar in appearance, but the tentacles are smooth, not knobby as they are in *Phymanthus*.

All are easy to keep, but coming as they do from very shallow water, need extremely bright light.

Bartholomea annulata, the Curleycue Anemone, is un-mistakable. Golden brown to cream colored, all speci-mens have rings of white spiraling around the tentacles, from which trait the common name of this species is derived.

This anemone will not only sting other anemones, it can eat them, as well, so beware. It can however be kept with the Flower and Rock anemones. It is worth keeping *Bartholomea* in a tank to itself, if only to enable one also to keep some of the interesting shrimps that live symbi-otically with it. See Chapter Eight for a discussion of these relationships.

The Antler Anemone, *Lebrunia danae*, is also unmistak-able. It has two types of tentacles, one set is short and closely circles the mouth, the other set is much larger and branches repeatedly, not unlike the antlers of a deer.

This is also known as the "Stinging Anemone" in south Florida. Beware. It is a pretty species, nonetheless, and can be kept with Curleycue and Flower anemones, as long as there is enough room to prevent actual contact. Various other anemones are available, from the Atlantic as well as the Indo-Pacific. The ones discussed above are those most often imported and most readily identified.

• **False Corals (Order** *Corallimorpharia***).**

The scientific name for this group of polyps means "coral shaped animals", but does not really describe them adequately. These are the "Mushroom Corals" of the aquarium industry.

All are basically flattened discs, with very short columns, and most occur in aggregations of several to many individuals. These are usually sold as groups of individuals attached to a rock.

Two species come from Florida, these are:

Ricordea florida, the Florida False Coral, once commonplace, is now difficult to obtain due to collecting restrictions in Florida waters. Polyps are usually about the size of a quarter, with bright green tentacles that are spherical, about 1/16 inch in diameter.

Occasionally, bright orange specimens are seen. Given bright light and excellent water quality, this species will reproduce in the aquarium, although it is sometimes reported as being difficult to keep.

Paradiscosoma elegans is commonly called the Neon Disc Anemone. It lives in inshore waters, usually on hardbottom areas where branched *Porites* corals, and many macroalgae, are found.

This is in contrast to *Ricordea*, which comes from deeper waters. This species is seldom collected for the aquarium, but well worth obtaining for its bright blue green coloration. Tentacles are absent.

Tentacles are absent from many of the Pacific "mushroom corals", of which there are several species from the genera *Rhodactis*, *Actinodiscus*, and *Discosoma*.

All are flat, rounded polyps with very short columns. Most mushroom corals do well in moderate light, and can be placed near the bottom of the aquarium, or in tanks where lighting is below 10,000 lux.

These false corals come in many colors, with blue-green, brown and green being the most common. Some have blue or red pigments, and are very striking. This pigmentation may change, however, if the lighting conditions in the tank are significantly different from those under which the specimen was growing in the ocean. As a general rule, the false corals are easy to keep, and will grow and multiply in the reef tank.

One other false coral deserves special mention. This is the Elephant Ear, a species of *Amplexidiscus*.

It is perhaps the largest of the false corals, reaching nearly a foot across, even under aquarium conditions that are less than perfect. Its only negative trait is a propensity to eat small fishes that may be unwary of its stubby tentacles.

Most other false corals rely either on photosynthesis entirely, or upon small planktonic organisms for their food.

• **Sea Mats (Order** *Zoantharia***)**.

This is an interesting and hardy group that lies somewhere between anemones and corals in the scheme of coelenterate classification.

Sea mats look like colonies of small anemones. In the

majority of species the polyps are all joined together at the base by a sheet of tissue that spreads over hard substrates and gives rise to additional polyps.

One in particular is not so connected, being classified with the sea mats because it shares other anatomical traits with them. This is *Parazoanthus axinellae*, sold as "Yellow Polyp Colony" in most shops.

This species is an excellent choice for the reef aquarium, and its bright lemon yellow color is both unusual and attractive. It is collected in the Indo-Pacific.

Hawaii was once the source of many other Pacific sea mats. These come in a variety of colors, but coloration is usually restricted to the center of the oral disc, with the column and tentacles being dull gray, brown, or greenish.

Colors range from greens to blue and even pink. Without a technical reference book, the Hawaiian species are difficult to identify, but seven species of sea mats may be available.

The most attractive is *Isaurus elongatus* which has polyps about two inches in length. In Isaurus, the dime-sized crown of tentacles is usually a lovely greenish-blue color.

Incidentally, the name *Isaurus elongatus* has incorrectly been applied to a tubeworm, the giant Hawaiian feather duster, in a number of publications. The correct name for this feather duster is *Sabellastarte sanctijosephi*. With such a tongue twister for a moniker, I am not surprised that the incorrect name for this worm has been used so often.

Palythoa vestitus, *P. psammophilia*, *P. toxica*, *Zoanthus pacificus* and *Z. kealakekuanensis* are also found in shipments from Hawaii.

Specimens of Hawaiian zoanthids are becoming less readily available, however, due to collecting restrictions in this state. However, very similar species are available from elsewhere in the Indo-Pacific, along with others that are not found in Hawaii.

I regularly see specimens that are green with orange centers, and a lovely pinkish-purple form, from Palau, for example.

Often Mushroom Coral specimens will have zoanthids present, in addition to the mushrooms themselves.

From the Atlantic and Caribbean comes the most commonly available of the sea mats, *Zoanthus sociatus*, or Green Sea Mat.

Although found in shallow inshore waters, this species may be so abundant on the back reef slope that ecologists have designated a "*Zoanthus* zone" on some reefs.

Other Atlantic zoanthids, including *Palythoa caribaea*, *P. tuberculosa*, and *Parazoanthus swifti*, are deep-reef organisms and thus are rarely found on sea mat rock from shallow water.

P. swifti is always found in association with sponges, and is thought by some authors to be a parasite. More likely, however, the association is a benign one, as I have never observed sponges harboring this sea mat that appeared to be harmed by the association in any way.

Given enough light, all sea mats are among the most easily kept reef invertebrates. Only *Parazoanthus swifti*, described above, needs feeding, and if you are feeding its sponge host, all should be well. The other species subsist almost entirely on photosynthesis carried out by their *zooxanthellae*.

• Soft Corals (Order *Alcyonaria*).

There are two large groups of "soft corals", which differ from all of the other coelenterates we have discussed, and from the true corals discussed below, in that their tentacles are always produced in multiples of eight.

Thus, the collective term used by biologists for this group of coelenterates is "*octocorals*". If you feel like counting tentacles, you can verify this fact for yourself.

The tentacles of all octocorals also differ in structure from those of the other groups, in that they have tiny branches along them that impart a feathery appearance.

Biologists divide this group into two subdivisions, and this is how we will consider them here. Classification of the subgroups is based upon the structure of the supporting skeleton, which in one group is stiffened, and in the other is composed of loose pieces of skeletal material.

Soft corals with a stiffened skeleton are gorgonians, commonly called sea fans and sea whips. There are a great many species of these, and they come in a wide variety of colors.

Sea whips are branched, like a leafless tree, while in sea fans the branches are fused together forming a network or mesh, resembling window screening. In all cases tiny polyps are arrayed along the branches; each gorgonian typically has hundreds of polyps.

The color of the polyps, and sometimes the color of the

skeleton, is an indication of the light requirements for gorgonians.

Those in which the polyps are brown or green in color require light, those with white, red or yellow polyps generally prefer shaded locations. Specimens in which the skeleton is red, orange or yellow are also generally found in the shade, while brownish, blue or purple skeletons typically belong to species that live out in the open sun.

Accurately determining the species of a particular gorgonian specimen may be quite difficult, but this should not matter to the aquarist, since all gorgonians have the same basic requirements.

Provide light for those that require it, and, in all cases, provide good water movement. Strong currents seem to be very important for these organisms.

Soft corals with "flabby" skeletons composed of loose aggregations of spicules are classified as "*alcyonarians*". Several of these are commonly imported for the aquarium.

Sarcophyton trocheliophorum, usually called Leather Mushroom Soft Coral, and a variety of related species, is among the most suitable of alcyonarians for a reef tank.

In all of the leather corals, the body mass is brownish or yellowish in color, and the polyps are embedded in this skeletal mass. Leather corals prefer high light intensities.

They often grow almost up to the surface of the ocean in nature. They also need a stable, high pH.

It is not unusual for the polyps of leather corals to remain contracted for several days after a change in water conditions, such as moving them from one aquarium to the other.

Starburst Soft Coral, *Clavularia viridis*, is also called Green Star Polyps, and is frequently misidentified as Organ Pipe Coral (*Tubipora musica*).

In this alcyonarian, the skeleton is a rubbery, flattened sheet that encrusts a solid substrate. Each polyp resides in a short tube that projects upward from the basal sheet about 1/4". The polyps themselves are generally pale green with bright green centers, or are an overall lime green color. When expanded, this is a very beautiful species.

It is also, happily, one of the hardiest and most durable of reef tank organisms, and can be highly recommended even to the beginner. Its only special requirement seems to be very bright light, under which it will grow and spread. It will even tolerate dim light, although in this situation it never looks at its best.

Several species of soft corals hold special interest for reef enthusiasts because they exhibit continuous, pulsing movements. These are collectively referred to as "pulse polyps", and may be species of either *Xenia* or *Anthelia*.

In the former, the columns of the individual polyps are long and thin, and the crown of tentacles reminds one of a daisy. They are brownish in color. In *Anthelia* the feathery, white polyps are attached at the base to form a cluster anchored to a rock or other hard surface.

The Manual of Marine Invertebrates indicates that both *Xenia* and *Anthelia* are hardy, easy to keep, and reproduce themselves readily in the aquarium.

Unfortunately, neither one is imported very frequently. Colt and Finger Soft Coral (*Cladiela sp. and Sinularia* sp.) are branched like a tree. Brown in color, with the "trunk" usually much lighter than the branches, these lovely species ha-ve requirements similar to *Sarcophyton*, described above.

Many other alcyonarians are imported for the aquarium. Most will require the same lighting and water conditions noted above for the leather corals. One exception is *Dendronephyta*, which I discussed in Chapter Nine. *Dendronephyta* prefers shade.

• **True Corals (Order** *Madreporaria***)**.

The true corals all produce a skeleton composed of calcium carbonate, a fact reflected in the other common name of this group, "stony" corals.

Accurate identification of corals may pose difficulties even for experts. Species available in the aquarium trade are readily recognizable and photographs of most of them have appeared at some time or another.

All corals require excellent water quality, with nitrates and phosphates at near zero concentration, and all except one require bright, broad spectrum lighting. The single exception to this rule is *Tubastrea*, the Orange Polyp Coral, which was discussed in Chapter Nine.

Following is a list of true corals available to aquarium hobbyists, with the correct scientific name, followed by as many of the common names as I could compile.

Consult reference books, such as *Corals of Australia and the Indo-Pacific* by J.E.N. Veron, or *Corals of the World*, by Elizabeth Wood, for excellent color photographs of all the species mentioned here.

I have included brief comments about many of the species, concerning their proper aquarium care.

Heliofungia actiniformis, Plate Coral, needs a soft, sandy substrate and plenty of room. It is not really suitable for the typical reef tank, but is spectacular in an aquarium designed with its special needs in mind. It is the only commonly available coral capable of moving from place to place.

Herpolitha limax, Slipper Coral, Hedgehog Coral, is a close relative of *Heliofungia* and needs similar conditions. Both these species are shallow water corals. Give them intense light and moderate, not forceful, current.

Goniopora lobata, Flowerpot Coral, Sunflower Coral, is considered difficult to maintain. This is because it demands top notch water quality and excellent light. In addition, it is easily damaged by careless handling.

If the polyps of your specimen do not expand nicely, there is too much organic matter in the water, or phosphates or nitrates are too high. A related genus, *Alveopora*, is almost indistinguishable from *Goniopora*, and is sometimes imported.

Trachyphyllia geoffreyi, Open Brain Coral, is a hardy and attractive species that is regularly imported. It is not a true brain coral. This coral is a single, large polyp. The skeleton is in the form of an inverted cone, attached, at the apex, to a hard substrate.

As a result of this growth form, this coral is easily removed without damage, which may explain why aquarium specimens do so well.

Cynaria species, Button Coral, is related to *Trachyphyllia* (see above), and should receive the same care.

Favia species, Closed Brain Coral, is unrelated either to *Trachyphyllia* or to the true brain corals. (True brain corals are seldom collected, although *Leptoria* is sometimes available, but costly.

Several kinds of *Favia* are imported. Make sure any specimen you select is a complete colony, not just a chunk hacked from a larger specimen. In the latter case, the aquarium lifespan of the specimen will be limited at best.

Turbinaria turbinata, Chalice Coral, Cup Coral, Wineglass Coral, is so named because the skeleton is shaped like a goblet with a very fat stem by which the coral is attached to a hard substrate.

Thin, brownish tissue covers the entire surface, so it is important to get a specimen still attached to a small piece of substrate, not one that has merely been snapped off above the point of attachment. The large, flowerlike polyps are borne only on the inside of the "goblet". *Turbinaria* is interesting in appearance, and easy to keep.

Plerogyra sinuosa, Bubble Coral, may be pale blue, brownish or green in color. This is a commonly available and popular species. Beware of damaged specimens, which rarely recover in the aquarium.

Bubble Coral will accept small bits of fish or shrimp as food, in addition to relying upon its *zooxanthellae* for sustenance. A related genus, *Physogyra*, which looks similar, is called Pearl Bubble Coral or Octopus Coral.

Several species of *Euphyllia* are available to aquarists, and all make good additions to the reef tank.

All have relatively long tentacles, and must not be

placed close to other invertebrates, which they may sting and nettle.

Common species include:

Euphyllia ancora, Anchor Coral, Hammerhead Coral, Hammer Coral, Ridge Coral, has a curved extension at the end of each tentacle, giving the appearance of little hammers or anchors.

Very desirable as an aquarium specimen, this *Euphyllia* should not be purchased if the skeleton is broken. ("Small" specimens may be sold as such because a batch of larger ones got broken in shipment. Beware.)

Euphyllia divisa, Wall Coral, Frogspawn Coral, Vase Coral, gets its colorful common name from the appearance of the tentacles. They sport numerous tubercles and white spots, suggesting a mass of frog's eggs when viewed at a distance. It is another good aquarium species.

Cataphyllia jardinieri, Tooth Coral, Elegance Coral, Elegant Coral, Meat Polyps, is closely related to *Euphyllia*. This is one of the most popular, hardy and spectacular true corals.

Like *Trachyphyllia* mentioned above, this species is easy to collect in undamaged condition. In addition, the polyps can withdraw completely into the skeleton, where they are adequately protected during transport, and the coral rarely arrives at its destination in damaged condition.

It is somewhat rare, however, and commands a premium price. However, if I were only going to have one coral, this would be my choice. Specimens can double in size in six months time.

All *Euphyllia* corals, as well as *Catalaphyllia*, can be fed small pieces of shrimp or fish, which will enhance their rate of growth.

They may also eat unwary gobies or other small fish. Do not, however, make the mistake of overfeeding, or feeding too frequently. Once a week is plenty, and giving no food at all does no harm.

All these species rely heavily upon their zooxanthellae, and can survive and grow with this food source alone.

One final note about true corals. They should never, repeat never, be removed from the water. Handle them very carefully, ideally with latex gloves.

Your dealer should wrap the specimen gently in a plastic bag, and place that inside a bag of water for transport. (Yes, all of this should be done under water.) Remember that a coral is basically a soft-bodied anemone with a sharp rock inside.

They are easy to damage, and even small amounts of damage can lead to fatal bacterial infections. To maximize your chances of success, buy live corals only from a dealer whom you know to be knowledgeable and experienced in the proper care of such organisms.

Apart from good light and high quality water, corals require calcium with which to construct their limy skeletons. Use a good quality calcium supplement to maintain the calcium concentration of the tank at 400 mg/liter. Calcium test kits are available.

The elements strontium and molybdenum are also required for deposition of the coral skeleton.

Specimens in which the polyps seem to be coming

"detached" from the skeleton may be lacking these two elements. Supplements are available to replenish strontium and molybdenum.

Unfortunately, it is not practical for the home aquarist to test for these elements, although the test can be done by a professional water analysis laboratory.

Corals and their relatives are some of the most beautiful and fragile of the reef's treasures. If you decide to keep them in the aquarium, treat them with the care and respect they deserve.

There is one other invertebrate that requires light, and it is not a coral. It is the Giant Clam, *Tridacna*, of which there are several species.

Overcollecting has reduced the numbers of these clams in the wild, and they are now protected throughout much of their natural range. Fortunately, tank raised giant clams are now available.

Of the seven or eight species of giant clams found in the Indo-Pacific region, six are available from the hatchery in Palau.

These are *Tridacna derasa*, *T. crocea*, *T. squamosa*, *T. gigas*, *T. maxima*, and *Hippopus hippopus*.

The recently described *Hippopus porcellanus*, and another newly discovered species of *Tridacna* have not yet appeared on the aquarium market as of the date of this writing.

The mantle of *Tridacna* is filled with *zooxanthellae*, which form interesting patterns that no doubt account for the appeal of this organism to aquarists. Coloration of the mantle ranges from bright green to blue and purple. Each individual clam looks a little different from every other, and all are quite beautiful.

The aquarium husbandry of all species of giant clams is the same. The clam relies exclusively upon its zooxanthellae for food. It absorbs both inorganic and organic nutrients from the water, probably for the primary benefit of the zooxanthellae.

Such nutrients include both ammonia and nitrate. Nitrate removal can be dramatic, if large numbers of clams are introduced into the tank. Phosphates are also absorbed. Thus, *Tridacna* actually enjoys levels of nitrate and phosphate that would be considered unsuitable for corals.

Nevertheless, attention should be paid to water quality for these clams, which require sufficient oxygen, a high, stable pH, and and alkalinity of 3.5 meq/l or more. A calcium supplement, such as "Kalkwasser", should be added to the aquarium on a regular basis.

Chapter Eleven

Macroalgae

How many times have you heard that macroalgae are difficult to grow? *Probably quite often*. There are many misconceptions about macroalgae and their requirements, and I would like to do what I can to dispel these misconceptions, as well as to identify the specimens you may see.

Macroalgae are fundamentally similar to the microalgae that form green and brown films on the glass and decorations in any aquarium. They are, however, more demanding in their requirements than are the microalgae, as we will soon see.

One common misconception concerning macroalgae is that they are appropriate specimens for a reef tank. This is not strictly true, as macroalgae such as *Caulerpa*, the most commonly available type, are rarely found on the reef.

Rather, macroalgae populate shallow water inshore habitats and lagoons, where they are relatively safe from herbivorous fishes such as tangs and angels.

Nevertheless, many aquarists include macroalgae in reef tanks to achieve a "natural" look .

A second misconception is that macroalgae will lower the nitrate concentration of the aquarium. This is only true in an indirect sense. While macroalgae will absorb nitrate, they preferentially absorb *ammonia*.

Thus, a tank with luxuriant macroalgae growth may generate less nitrate only because removal of ammonia by the macroalgae makes the ammonia unavailable for processing by the biological filter. Less ammonia into the system at the "front end" means less nitrate production.

A third misconception is that macroalgae are to be avoided because they will invariably die and release harmful compounds into the water, spelling disaster for all of the tank's other inhabitants. This notion is a mix of both fact and fiction.

In the first place, only *Caulerpa* species experience mass "die-off" with any regularity.

This phenomenon is associated with the reproductive cycle, or sporulation, of the algae. I have seen it occur only once with a species other than a member of the *Caulerpa* genus; in that instance, the species was *Halimeda discoidea*.

In any case, sporulation can be avoided by proper maintenance techniques, about which I will have more to say below.

As to the assertion that harmful compounds are released, again, this is a mixture of both fact and fiction. Many macroalgae produce poisonous alkaloids to deter other organisms from feeding upon them.

Also, the death and decay of any organism will create pollution in the aquarium if the filtration system's capacity is overloaded.

However, I suspect that the most likely explanation for disastrous effects upon the other specimens in the tank, following a sporulation event by *Caulerpa*, is the result of oxygen depletion.

The "spore" of *Caulerpa* is a free-swimming organism that may be considered to be analogous to a mammalian sperm cell. It swims vigorously by means of a whip-like appendage, the flagellum. This activity demands plenty of oxygen.

Since literally millions of these "spores" may be released at once, enough to tint the water green, oxygen depletion can occur, and fish and other organisms can die as a result of oxygen starvation.

There are three major groups into which macroalgae are classified by biologists. These groups may be thought of, for our purposes, as based upon the pigmentation of the most common members of each group.

By far the most familiar are the green algae, (*Chlorophyta*), with *Caulerpa* being a typical species. Red algae (*Rhodophyta*) are typified by species such as *Gracillaria*. (Note that the "red slime" algae that sometime reach plague proportions in the aquarium are in this group).

The third group, brown algae (*Phaeophyta*), includes the giant kelps and numerous other species that live in cool waters, although there are several tropical species, notably *Sargassum*.

The ideal arrangement for the aquarist who wishes to

grow macroalgae (a laudable goal, in my opinion, since macroalgae are very beautiful), is to set up a tank just for the purpose, and to populate it with invertebrates and fishes that would normally be found in the same shallow water habitats in which macroalgae are commonly found.

Such a tank would not be a "reef tank" in the sense that the term is used by most authors, but would neverthe-less have the same kind of filtration system and lighting.

Some species of macroalgae, those that are indeed found in true reef habitats, can be included in a reef tank with corals and other invertebrates, if this suits your taste.

Let us consider the macroalgae species that would be most appropriate for the "classic" reef tank. Then, we will turn our attention to designing a habitat tank dominated by macroalgae. Finally, we will cover the techniques of caring for the special needs of these marine "plants".

Halimeda is the most common macroalgae genus on many reefs in the Caribbean and Florida. There are several species, by far the most common of which is *H. opuntia*. *H. discoidea*, *H. incrassata*, and *H. tuna* are also commonly collected. All four species are usually sold simply as "*Halimeda*".

The body of *Halimeda* is composed of flat, calcified plates or discs that are attached together at the edges.

The shape of the individual disc is useful in identifying the species. *H. incrassata* produces a stalked structure that looks a lot like the Saguaro cactus of the American southwest, if you have a vivid imagination.

This species is usually anchored in the substrate by its

holdfast, while the other three *Halimeda* species are usually attached to rocks, or form loose clumps that simply lie on the substrate or scramble over boulders and rubble.

H. opuntia is most commonly found in clumps that grow in cracks or spaces between rocks on the reef. This is the growth form that is most easily duplicated in the reef tank. Because of the calcareous skeleton, *Halimeda* is seldom eaten by tangs and angelfishes.

Dictyosphaerium cavernosum is the second species that can be found on the reef. It is easy to identify, as it looks like a mass of green golf balls attached to a rock. The individual spheres that make up a clump of *Dictyosphaerium* are in turn formed of numerous smaller spheres, giving the overall "dimpled" appearance of a golf ball.

This species has proven easy to keep in the aquarium, and is not bothered by tangs, who seem unable to bite off chunks from the smooth, rounded colony. (It may be unpalatable for other reasons, as well.)

Avrainvillea nigricans is sold under the name of Velvet Fan Plant, or sometimes simply Velvet Plant. These common names aptly describe this macroalga, which feels as though it were indeed made of green velvet.

Specimens may be almost black in color when initially collected, but new growth that develops in the aquarium will be bright green. It is found either rooted in the substrate, or attached to a rock. The latter form is more desirable for the reef tank, but may be difficult to obtain.

It is not eaten by fishes, despite its soft texture, and thus may be poisonous, or at least foul tasting. The only other macroalga that looks superficially similar to *Avrainvillea* are *Udotea species*, which is stiff and calcified (see below).

Another assortment of macroalgae species may occur on live rock specimens.

These are often rather small, but may be quite beautiful. Among the most common ones are several species of mauve or purple calcareous red algae that encrust rocks from deeper waters.

Given aquarium conditions to their liking, these algae will reproduce in the tank, encrusting even the glass and other objects. They never reach plague proportions, however, and the overall effect is very attractive, at least to me.

Among the green macroalgae found on live rocks, *Dasycladus vermicularis*, which looks like 3-inch lengths of green pipe cleaners clustered together, and *Batophora*, a relative of *Dasycladus* that looks like clusters of small, green bananas, are frequently present.

One other genus that you are likely to see on live rock specimens is *Dictyota*, a member of the brown algae family. One species, *Dictyota dichotoma*, seems to be quite common. Its golden brown fronds divide repeatedly, producing a loose clump held upright above the point of attachment.

Dictyota is probably the most commonly seen member of the brown algae family in tropical habitats. Its "cousin", *Sargassum*, is only occasionally seen, and is very difficult to cultivate in the aquarium.

One other brown alga genus deserves mention. This is *Padina*, which must be obtained attached to a rock if there is to be any hope of keeping this fussy species alive in the tank. It lives in shallow inshore waters, where it forms clumps of ruffled, fan-shaped blades attached to rocks and rubble.

The blades are golden brown in color, with alternating bands of bright yellow-green. It is an attractive species, but has so far defied my best attempts to get it to survive for more than a month or two.

I have observed that *Padina* does not retain its banded appearance in the aquarium, and this may be related to its failure to grow. Perhaps some essential nutrient is lacking.

When you obtain live rock specimens harboring any of the macroalgae mentioned above, they can make very desirable additions to the reef tank.

However, if you are interested in the widest variety and abundance of macroalgae species, I suggest you set up a shallow water tank, for it is in this habitat that the diversity of macroalgae is greatest.

For our purposes, the macroalgae of shallow inshore waters may be divided into two groups: those that produce a calcium carbonate skeleton, and those that do not.

In general, the members of the latter group are easier to grow. By far the most commonly available are members of the large genus *Caulerpa*. *C. prolifera* and *C. mexicana* will be available from any dealer that stocks macroalgae.

C. prolifera has a simple flat blade that often spirals like a loose corkscrew as it grows upward. *C. mexicana* has a blade more reminiscent of a fern frond, that is, it is deeply notched.

Less common species include *C. racemosa*, in which the blade looks like a bunch of grapes (hence the common name "grape *Caulerpa*").

C. peltata, which has a blade consisting of an upright central stem with little lollipop-shaped "leaflets" attached along its length, *C. sertularoides*, with a blade that looks like a bird's feather, and *C. verticillata*, or "dwarf *Caulerpa*, with short blades composed of a central filament bearing tufts of side filaments arranged in whorls along its length.

All these species of *Caulerpa* are adapted to scrambling over rubble, dead coral heads, and similar hard, irregular substrates.

Arrange the plants attractively on top of a rock positioned in good light, and they will soon attach themselves and begin to grow.

Several other species of *Caulerpa* are adapted to life in sandy or muddy habitats. These include *C. paspaloides*, which produces a tall stiff blade crowned with feathery branches that give the overall appearance of a palm tree, *C. cupressoides*, with tough, squarish blades that are toothed along the edges, and *C. lanuginosa*, the blade of which is a fat, rounded rod covered with little projections that give it the appearance of the branch of a spruce tree.

These three species require a fine substrate material in which to grow. Under optimum conditions, growth of *Caulerpa* species can be as much as an inch a day, so pruning will be necessary.

The prunings can be fed to fish (tangs and angels love to eat *Caulerpa*), or can be used to start new plants.

A single blade of *any species of Caulerpa* can be partially buried in sand, and will form a complete new plant within a few weeks.

Pruning seems to be important in preventing *Caulerpa* from undergoing sporulation, a process described above. Natural growths of *Caulerpa* are probably "pruned" regularly by algae-eating animals.

The calcareous varieties are among the most interesting and beautiful macroalgae.

This group includes the various species of *Halimeda*, mentioned above, which are found in shallow water habitats as well as on the reef. Others include Merman's Shaving Brush (*Penicillus capitatus* and *P. dumetosus*), the appearance of which is adequately described by the common name.

Green Sea Fan is the name most frequently given to species of *Udotea* (two species are available, *U. spinulosa*, a flattened form, and *U. cyathiformis*, in which the "fan" is curved, almost cone shaped).

Sea Paintbrush or Pinecone Shaving Brush are two common names that describe the appearance of *Rhipocephalus phoenix*.

My favorite calcareous macroalga, however, is *Cymopolia barbata*. It looks like branched strings of white beads with a tuft of green filaments forming a "pom-pom" at the tip of each branch.

All of the calcareous macroalgae grow best if obtained attached to a rock, although they also grow in loose, sandy substrates. Each of the species mentioned above has an upright stalk, with a rootlike structure, the holdfast, at the lower end.

The holdfast anchors the plant in the substrate, or to a hard surface, and does not function as the roots of terrestrial plants do.

Calcareous algae often appear in shipments with the holdfast missing. Such plants will not survive for long. Look for specimens, if not attached to a rock, that have obviously been dug, rather than pulled up or broken off.

All of the species of *Caulerpa*, and all of the calcareous macroalgae discussed above, can form the basis of an aquarium mimicking the shallow waters of a lagoon.

Other organisms that would be found in such a habitat in the Florida Keys, for example, include *Condylactis* anemones, many varieties of gorgonians, sea cucumbers, brittle stars, snails, sea slugs, shrimps, crabs and the ever popular seahorse.

Many fishes live in this habitat, also. Juveniles of many reef dwelling species seek food and shelter in shallow waters. Other species, such as lizardfishes, rays, and stargazers make their permanent homes among the seaweeds, but few of these are ever collected for the aquarium.

Organisms that feed upon *Caulerpa* and the other algae are also abundant in this habitat, of course, but one would not put these in an aquarium devoted to growing macroalgae.

The single most important requirement for the cultivation of macroalgae is sufficient *light*. Refer to Chapter Three for information regarding selection of lighting systems for the aquarium.

The optimum light intensity for most tropical macroalgae is about 16,000 lux. Most can survive on less, but will

grow poorly.   The second requirement for success with
macroalgae is adequate nutrition.   The major and minor
nutrients required by macroalgae are: nitrogen compounds, phosphate, potassium, sulfate, iron, manganese, thiamine, biotin, and vitamin B-12.

Nitrogen compounds and phosphate are generally always available in the aquarium, often to the extent that
we must take measures to remove them.

Other major elements (potassium, sulfate, and manganese) are present in seawater mixes. Iron, an important
trace element for macroalgae growth, must be replen-
ished on a regular basis. Iron depletion is a major factor
in sporulation of *Caulerpa*, as described above.

To insure that your macroalgae specimens are getting
enough iron, you should test the water regularly with an
iron test kit. Based on your test results, add an iron
supplement to the water to maintain a concentration of
0.05 to 0.1 mg/l. You may need to add iron supplement
as frequently as every other day, if your plants are
growing well.

There are several commercially available trace element
supplements that contain iron, such as those made by
Coralife and Thiel-Aqua-Tech.

Tests for biotin, thiamine and vitamin B-12 cannot be
carried out by the home hobbyist, unless you have an
analytical laboratory in your basement.

Supplements are available, however, that are made
specifically to supply these vitamins for macroalgae.

If you have the facilities, and access to the chemicals,
you might want to prepare your own supplements.

The formulas that have worked for me are as follows:

VITAMIN SUPPLEMENT FOR MACROALGAE
Thiamine hydrochloride   2.00 grams
Biotin   0.01 grams
Cyanocobalamin (B-12)   0.01 grams
Glass distilled water   1000.00 milliliters

This supplement is used weekly at the rate of 3.8 ml per gallon of tank water. Store it in the refrigerator.

IRON-MANGANESE SUPPLEMENT FOR MACROALGAE
Iron (ferric) citrate dihydrate   3.83 grams
Manganese chloride   0.02 grams
Trisodium Ethylenediamine-tetra-acetate   7.60 grams
Glass distilled water   1000.00 ml

This supplement is added as required to maintain a concentration of iron at 0.05 mg/l in the tank. Start with 3.8 ml of supplement per gallon of tank water.

The final requirement for growing macroalgae successfully is proper maintenance. This includes all the maintenance procedures and water changes that you would carry out with any reef tank, as well as regular pruning of *Caulerpa*, as mentioned above.

Algae which have calcareous skeletons extract calcium from the water, and are especially sensitive to a decline in pH. Test pH and alkalinity regularly, adding one of the commercially available carbonate hardness supplements as required.

Provide a calcium supplement as well, added according to the manufacturer's directions. There are now quite a few on the market.

Some fishes and invertebrates are not compatible with macroalgae. Tangs, angelfishes, sea urchins, and many mollusks will readily consume your carefully tended underwater garden, so avoid these animals if you plan to grow macroalgae.

No books devoted to the aquarium culture of macroalgae are yet available, but here are two suggestions for further reading on this fascinating topic:

Bold, H.C. and M.J. Wynne (1978) *Introduction to the Algae*. Prentice-Hall, Inglewood Cliffs, New Jersey. 706 pp. A college textbook dealing with all aspects of the biology of marine and freshwater algae.

Taylor, W. Randolph (1960) *Marine Algae of the Tropical and Subtropical Coasts of the Americas*. University of Michigan Press, Ann Arbor. 870 pp. The most comprehensive and authoritative guide to identification of the species of the region covered.

Fortunately, many species of macroalgae are worldwide in their distribution, so this book is useful for the Indo-Pacific macroalgae, also. It is lavishly illustrated with line drawings, making it easy for the non-professional to use.

Both of these books are college-level texts. You can find brief discussions on macroalgae in many books devoted to reef aquariums, and in field guides.

Also seek out *Seaweeds of Hawaii*, by William H. Magruder and Jeffrey W. Hunt (Oriental Publishing Company, Hawaii), and *Marine Plants of the Caribbean—a Field Guide From Florida to Brazil*, by Diane S. Littler, Mark M. Littler, Katina E. Bucher, and James N. Norris (Smithsonian Institution Press, Washington), for excellent color photographs of tropical macroalgae from these two regions of the world. Again, these books are useful for identifying species from outside the ranges they cover.

In summary, macroalgae make good additions to the reef tank, but are best enjoyed in a habitat tank devoted to them and the fish and invertebrates that live with them in nature.

Macroalgae require good light, adequate nutrition, and proper aquarium maintenance in order to thrive. Once established, however, most algae reproduce themselves rapidly, freeing the aquarist from dependency upon wild-collected specimens. This fact should be noted by hobbyists concerned with conservation of marine organisms.

They will reward the careful aquarist with a beautiful diversity of form and color, and are, in my opinion, much underappreciated by aquarium hobbyists.

I hope this book will help to change that situation.

Chapter Twelve

Crustaceans

We will complete our discussion of reef tank inverte-brates with a look at the crustaceans. Many varieties of crustaceans are readily available to any aquarist.

Our primary concern will be with the compatibility of various species with the other invertebrates present in the reef tank, and with each other.

Crustaceans belong to the largest of invertebrate groups, the arthropods. This huge assemblage includes all or-ganisms with jointed appendages, an exoskeleton com-posed of chitin (a tough, but flexible protein similar to fingernails), and a segmented body.

The most commonly recognized terrestrial arthropods are the insects and spiders, but in the ocean, it is the crustaceans that are the dominant group.

The crustacean group includes brine shrimp, amphi-pods, copepods, mantis shrimps, true shrimps, hermit crabs, true crabs, and lobsters, along with several other types of marine arthropods of little interest to the aquar-ist. Brine shrimp are familiar as a food source for many types of aquarium organisms. Amphipods and copepods are seldom added to the aquarium deliberately as specimens, but these tiny, shrimp-like creatures often turn up in tanks that have been established for several months, and frequently cause concern because they may undergo a population explosion in the tank.

This concern is unwarranted, for these organisms are harmless. Their presence in the aquarium may indicate that detritus is accumulating, for it is upon this material that they feed, but otherwise the appearance of amphipods and copepods in the aquarium should be no cause for alarm.

True, there are parasitic forms of both these types of crustaceans, but such parasites will always be attached to their host organism (usually a fish), and not crawling about on the glass or rocks.

Many fishes feed upon amphipods and copepods. Among these are mandarins and seahorses, about which we will have more to say in Chapter Thirteen.

Mantis shrimps are another type of crustacean that may turn up unexpectedly in the aquarium. They usually come in hidden in a crevice or hole in a piece of live rock. Many are harmless, but all are predatory, and should be removed if possible.

They can be tricky to catch, but if you can locate the mantis shrimp's lair in the rocks, you can sometimes extract the shrimp with a wire hook. Failing this, it may be necessary to remove the entire rock to a bucket of seawater, which will give you a better opportunity to extract the shrimp.

I emphasize, however, that the presence of a single small mantis shrimp in the tank is hardly cause for panic.

Drastic measures should be taken only if you determine for certain that the mantis shrimp has actually done some damage to one of your specimens.

Mantis shrimp are active mostly at night, and this is a good time to observe the tank for their presence. You can find pictures of mantis shrimps in most books devoted to marine invertebrates, and in this way learn to recognize them.

The particular species you have is not important, as all look basically similar in body form. If you find that you do indeed have a large, destructive mantis shrimp, do not attempt to handle it bare-handed. Some can lash out with their feeding appendages and cause a nasty cut.

One large species found in temperate seas is called "thumb splitter" by fishermen, who use them for bait.

Among the crustaceans of most interest to aquarists, then, we have the hermit crabs, true crabs, true shrimp, and lobsters. Let us consider each of these groups in turn.

• Hermit Crabs.

All hermit crabs protect themselves living in the discarded shell of a dead snail. There are many species, and most from the tropics are colorful. Being very hardy, hermit crabs are often the first invertebrate that is kept by the beginning aquarist.

A few hermit crabs can be included in any marine aquarium, and make excellent scavengers.

Make sure that the species you are considering is not one that grows large, however, since large hermits can be destructive.

Suitable species that are commonly available include *Calcinus tibicen*, *Calliactis tricolor*, *Paguristes cadenati*, and *Pagurus operculatus*, all from Florida and the Caribbean; *Aniculus strigatus*, *Calcinus latens*, and *C. elegans* are imported from Hawaii.

These hermit crabs are pictured in various marine invertebrate books.

• True Crabs.

Only a few of the true crabs are suitable for the reef aquarium, since most crabs are too large, too boisterous, too destructive, or too secretive to be of interest. Three species are worth mentioning, however.

From the Atlantic comes the Arrow Crab, *Stenorhynchus seticornis*, which looks like a spider with its long, spindly legs. The name comes from the arrowhead shape of the body.

Two arrow crabs cannot be kept together, as they will fight to the death, with the winner making a meal of the loser. The arrow crab does not get along well with Banded Coral Shrimp, either (see below).

Despite its untrustworthiness in the presence of these other crustaceans, the arrow crab can be a useful addition to the tank, as it will seek out and eliminate pesky bristleworms, which it eats.

Its fondness for polychaetes extends to the more desirable species, however, and this crab should be avoided if you intend to keep large feather dusters and the like.

The unrelated Decorator Arrow Crab, *Podochela reisi*, also comes from the tropical Atlantic. Like several other species of crabs, *Podochela* camouflages its body by attaching bits of living organisms, such as sponges and algae, to its carapace.

Thus, it may pick off small organisms from live rock, but really does no severe damage. Each time the crab molts, it will don a new set of "clothes", since the camouflage is shed along with the crab's exoskeleton.

It may remove some of its favorite attire from the cast off exoskeleton, and reattach these, or it may select an entirely new ensemble from whatever is at hand. The amusing behavior of *Podochela* is well worth the loss of a few live rock organisms.

Podochela, like *Stenorhynchus*, will feed on polychaete worms, but either species will also scavenge for food. Neither seems to harm corals, anemones, or other coelenterates.

Perhaps the most interesting of all invertebrates is a crab. This is the Pom Pom Crab, *Lybia edmonsoni*, from Hawaii. A similar species found elsewhere in the Indo-Pacific, *L. dubia*, has been described, but these two names may refer to the same animal.

In any case, *Lybia* presents a very rare example of tool-use among invertebrates. The crab has specially modified claws in which it grasps two tiny sea anemones, *Triactis producta*. In Hawaii, this anemone species is found only with the crab, but it does occur in the absence of the crab in other localities, including Australia, India, and the Red Sea.

The crab uses the anemones as mops, to gather detritus and other crab edibles, which cling to the anemone's tentacles.

When threatened, the crab puts its anemones to another use, brandishing them as weapons. The stinging tentacles of the anemone are sufficient to ward off most of the crab's enemies, apparently. Interestingly, it is not known for certain if the anemone benefits from this relationship.

Certainly the anemone obtains bits of food, as a natural consequence of its role in the feeding behavior of the crab.

Free-living specimens of *Triactis* are a rich golden-brown color, and contain *zooxanthellae*. When carried by *Lybia*, however, the anemone turns pale brown or white, and loses its *zooxanthellae*, because the secretive crab spends much of its time hidden under rocks and in crevices, away from the light.

My own observations seem to indicate that the anemones eventually die under these circumstances. Specimens of *Lybia* kept in my own aquarium have lost their anemones after several months, despite the presence of abundant food.

Presumably, if this happens to the crab in a region of the world where the anemones are free-living, the crab has only to locate another pair.

But what about Hawaii, where the anemones are never found unless in the crab's possession? *Triactis* gives birth to living offspring, so it is possible that reproduction may occur in the anemone during its captivity, thus providing the crab with a steady supply, but I have found no information on this topic during my reading on the subject.

Finding out more about this extremely interesting relationship would be a useful goal for keeping *Lybia* in the aquarium.

I mention it here because this species is quite suitable for the reef tank, but *Lybia* and its anemone "tools" really belong in a small tank devoted just to them.

The secretive habits of the crab result in its being seen only occasionally if placed in a large tank.

• Anemone Crabs.

The anemone crabs are close relatives of the true crabs, but with important differences. First, while true crabs are often scavengers, anemone crabs are filter feeders.

They have specially modified legs that are used to sweep the water for floating debris and plankton. Second, as the name implies, anemone crabs are found with anemones.

The two species usually imported for the aquarium associate with giant anemones, such as *Stoicactis* and other clownfish host species. Sometimes clownfish will live peaceably with an anemone crab sharing the anemone, and sometimes not.

In the latter case, the crab is evicted by the clownfish, and usually does poorly thereafter if another suitable anemone host cannot be found.

If you wish to keep clownfish and anemone crabs in the same tank, it is wise to provide two anemones, in case the clownfish becomes overly possessive.

The most commonly available anemone crab is *Petrolisthes maculatus*, with an attractive pattern of wine-red polka dots on its otherwise white carapace. Less frequently seen is *P. oshimani*, with many fine red dots scattered uniformly over its back and claws.

Mated pairs of both species are sometimes available, and will share an anemone.

• Lobsters.

Few lobsters are suitable for any aquarium, and those that are suitable should be avoided in the reef tank, as they grow to an unwieldy size, and cannot be trusted to leave their tankmates unharmed.

In addition, they are generally secretive, and spend most of their time out of sight. Spiny lobsters, in the genus *Panulirus*, are reasonably well-behaved, but do spend most of their time in hiding, emerging only at night to feed.

For aquarium purposes, only *P. versicolor*, the blue spiny lobster, is obtainable. Fishing regulations prohibit the taking of *P. argus*, the Florida spiny lobster or "crawfish", at a size small enough for the typical tank.

• Shrimps.

Among the crustaceans, the widest variety of species suitable for the reef aquarium is found among the shrimps.

For our purposes, we can divide the many members of this group into two categories: those that are free-living, and those that associate with anemones or other organisms. The free-living shrimps are easier to keep, and we will discuss them first.

Probably the most common shrimp in aquarium shops is the Banded Coral Shrimp, *Stenopus hispidus*. *Stenopus* species are placed in the Family *Stenopodidae* by biologists. This species, with its huge claws, red and white stripes, and long white antennae, is hardy and undemanding. On the reef, *Stenopus* is a cleaner, but this behavior is rarely exhibited in the aquarium, and the shrimp is content to feed upon stray bits of food missed by the fishes.

Mated pairs of Banded Coral Shrimp are sometimes available. Having a mated pair is the only way to keep two of these shrimps together, as they will fight to the death otherwise.

Recent studies indicate that females will accept any male in the neighborhood, however, if he is introduced immediately after she molts. The shrimps can be sexed reliably, thanks to the work of Justin Strynchuk, as reported in the October 1990 issue of *Freshwater and Marine Aquarium*.

Dealers and hobbyists alike should check out this article if interested in obtaining a mated pair of *S. hispidus*. I can only assume that Mr. Strynchuck's methods would also work for the other members of the genus *Stenopus*, which are from time to time available to aquarists.

These include *S. scutellatus*, the Golden Banded Coral Shrimp from the Atlantic, and *S. pyrsonotus*, the rare and expensive Ghost Cleaner Shrimp, from Hawaii.

In nature, *Stenopus hispidus*, often shares its territory with another cleaner shrimp, the Scarlet Lady, *Lysmata grabhami*. Unlike *Stenopus*, the Scarlet Lady Shrimp is not aggressive toward members of its own species, and a dozen or more of these interesting shrimps can be kept in the same tank.

Scarlet Lady Shrimp, also known as "Scarlet Cleaner" and "Eel Cleaner" shrimp, will eat a variety of common aquarium foods, and usually subsist quite well by scavenging. They are avid cleaners, however, and will even alight the hand of the aquarist, tugging at hairs, and removing bits of dead tissue from around the finger-nails.

Fish that are, to the aquarist's eye, free from external parasites and wounds will nevertheless seek out the services of the Scarlet Cleaner Shrimp in the aquarium.

Cleaning behavior is practiced by a number of fish and invertebrate species, and has obvious advantages to both the cleaner and the individual being cleaned. If you decide to keep a Scarlet Lady Shrimp or two in your reef tank, you can keep any of the other shrimps mentioned below along with them.

However, do not trust the Banded Coral Shrimp, or other members of the genus *Stenopus* with other, smaller shrimps. I would not place a Scarlet Lady in a small tank with a large Arrow Crab, either.

Lysmata grabhami is in Family *Hippolytidae*. Several other members of this family are available for the aquarium. *L. wurdemanni*, for example, is called the Peppermint Shrimp or Candycane Shrimp, and is very common in Florida and the Caribbean.

It is usually found around sponges or other encrusting invertebrates, and exhibits cleaning behavior. It grows to about 1 1/2" in length, and is transparent with bright red markings. It is apparently not difficult to catch, as specimens are seldom expensive.

Several authors have recommended keeping a few peppermint shrimps in any reef tank, because they regularly mate in captivity, producing an abundance of free-swimming larvae that can serve as a nutritious food for filter feeders. *However, this little shrimp renders a far more valuable service*. It eats *Aiptasia*, those pesky little brown anemones that can multiply to almost plague proportions in some reef tanks.

Many authors recommend eliminating *Aiptasia* whenever possible, citing their ability to "nettle" other coelenterates. If *Aiptasia* do greatly increase in numbers, they can pose a hazard. I have heard a number of recommendations for eliminating *Aiptasia*, although none are really practical.

For example, you can inject each individual anemone with potassium chloride. This will certainly do them in, but is an extremely tedious undertaking. Simply pulling or scraping them off the glass and rocks does no good, since even a tiny piece of the anemone's basal disk will regenerate an entire new individual in a few weeks time. (If only bright green carpet anemones were so easy to cultivate!)

Other suggestions include introducing a Copperband or Raccoon butterflyfish, waiting until all the *Aiptasia* have been eaten, and then devising a way to catch the fish again before it starts feeding on your corals.

I am told that German aquarists actually set up tanks and deliberately cultivate abundant *Aiptasia* for use as "training camps" for immature Copperband Butterflies destined for duty as *Aiptasia* removers in the reef tank.

The theory behind this is that the butterflyfish, having learned to feed only on *Aiptasia*, will continue this practice once moved from the "training camp" to the front lines. This seems to me like a lot of trouble for an approach that may not always work.

Further, if it does not work there is the problem of extracting the agile butterflyfish from the carefully arranged reef tank, with all those crannies and caves.

Enthusiasm dims at the prospect of trying to catch any fish, much less a butterflyfish, under such circumstances.

At any rate, the common, cheap little Peppermint Shrimp will do the job, and you do not have to worry about them starting in on your Elegance Coral after the *Aiptasia* are all gone.

I learned about this quite by accident , when a customer returned to my store with two Peppermint Shrimp he had recently purchased. He was a little irate, complaining that the shrimp had eaten all of his "little brown anemones", of which he was quite fond, since he had grown them himself.

I assured him that we were unaware of the propensity of the shrimp to consume the anemones, took back the shrimp, and sent him happily on his way with as many *Aiptasia* as we could find in the store.

He was so pleased to get more anemones that he did not even want his money back for the shrimp; we just made an even swap. I placed the Peppermint Shrimp in a tank with *Aiptasia*, and sure enough, the anemone population gets smaller every day. Sir, if you are reading this, my heartfelt thanks.

Peppermint Shrimp do not seem able to deal with large *Aiptasia*. It would be wise to add the shrimp shortly after you have added all of the live rock to your tank, if you do not want *Aiptasia* to gain a foothold.

Another hippolytid shrimp, *Thor amboinensis*, is probably not a cleaner, but is always found in association with anemones. In the Atlantic, it associates with the Curleycue Anemone, *Bartholomea annulata* and the Atlantic Carpet Anemone, *Stoicactis helianthus*.

It is sometimes referred to as "Sexy Shrimp", and occurs in the Indo-Pacific as well as the Atlantic and Caribbean. These delightful little shrimp were once readily available, but now, alas, are rarely imported.

If you are lucky enough to obtain a specimen, remember that it must, like all other anemone shrimp, be kept with an appropriate host. In the Indo-Pacific, this shrimp associates with corals as well as various anemones.

Most anemone shrimp species belong to Family *Palaemonidae*, and to a single genus, *Periclimenes*. If you obtain any of these shrimps, remember that they must be kept with an appropriate host.

The best approach is to purchase the shrimp and its host anemone together. Mated pairs of these shrimps are sometimes available, and the two will share a single anemone. Otherwise, attempting to keep two shrimp in a single anemone may result in a territorial squabble.

Three species occur in the Atlantic, but only two of these are imported with any regularity. Pederson's Cleaning Shrimp, *Periclimenes pedersoni*, occurs on *Bartholomea*, perching in the tentacles and swaying back and forth to attract "customers".

It rarely leaves the anemone, except to carry out its cleaning services. The body of this shrimp is transparent, with attractive white and purple markings. Like most cleaners, it has white antennae. It grows to just over an inch in length.

P. yucatanensis is a bit larger, also transparent, and is marked with distinctive tan and white saddles on the back of its carapace. The legs are banded in white and purple, and there is a series of purple dots, surrounded with white circles, along the sides of the abdomen and on the upper surface of the tail. The antennae are white, but there is no direct evidence that *P. yucatanensis* is actually a cleaner. It may be a "false cleaner", mimicking the behavior in order to benefit from the relative protection from predation that true cleaner shrimps enjoy.

Fish rarely eat cleaners, as the latter provide a valuable service on the reef. *P. yucatanensis* associates with *Bartholomea*, as well as *Condylactis gigantea*, the Haitian Pink Tipped Anemone, and with the Antler Anemone, *Lebrunia danae*.

Several species of *Periclimenes* are imported from the Pacific. *P. brevicarpalis* is associated with anemones, and is similar in appearance to *P. yucatanensis*, with distinctive white saddles along the back.

It differs in having orange, rather than purple, circles, surrounded by black, on the top of each tail segment. These orange spots are distinctive, and make identification easy. Males are much smaller than females, and are pale in color. In the females the white saddles are quite obvious, in males they are present, but not immediately noticeable.

P. brevicarpalis has blue or purple antennae, and is not thought to be a cleaner. It may be a false cleaner, like its cousin, *P. yucatanensis*.

P. holthusii is seldom seen in the aquarium trade, but should be sought out. It is attractively marked in red and white dots. It has white antennae, and may be a cleaner. It is found in association with large anemones, as well as Plate Coral (*Heliofungia actiniformis*).

This shrimp has the amusing habit of holding its chelae ("pincers") in position and moving them back and forth as if it were cradling a baby. This has earned it the common name of Rockabye Baby Shrimp.

The most spectacular, and most expensive, of the Indo-Pacific species is the Fire Shrimp or Blood Shrimp, *Lysmata debelius*.

Bright red in color, it bears four pairs of white polka dots, one pair between the eyes, another pair just behind and below the eyes, a third pair centered on the thorax, and a fourth pair on the first abdominal segment. The tips of the legs and the antennae are white. It is probably a cleaner.

One reason that the Fire Shrimp commands a high price is that it does not ship well, and many probably die en route from collectors to this country. Those that survive are marked up to compensate for the losses in transit.

Dealers must pay a higher price than for most other shrimps, and this is reflected in the retail price tag. Once settled into the aquarium, however, the shrimp is hardy and gets along with its tankmates.

Ironically, I have learned that Fire Shrimp ship quite well if provided with about twice the volume of water required by most other shrimp species. This suggests that they are sensitive to the build-up wate that occurs in the shipping water.

I have said before, and I repeat here, if more attention were paid to little details like this when shipping fish and invertebrates from reef habitats to dealers, a lot more animals would arrive in better condition.

Not only would this mean increased success for the hobbyist, but also fewer losses along the way would translate into more stable prices at the retail level.

There are literally thousands of species of crustaceans.

Those I have discussed here are generally available, attractive, interesting, and suitable for the reef tank. Some, like the Pom Pom Crab, are fascinating enough to merit a tank of their own.

One species not covered is the Curleycue Shrimp, *Alpheus armatus*, which was discussed in detail in Chapter Eight.

This species is a snapping shrimp, Family *Alpheidae*.

Several other *alpheid* shrimps are of interest, especially those that associate with certain species of Indo-Pacific gobies.

These will be covered in the next chapter, when we take up the subject of fishes for the reef tank.

Chapter Thirteen

Fishes for the Reef Tank

This chapter is not so much about all of the types of fishes that can be kept in the reef aquarium, but rather about establishing a harmonious community of fishes in a tank that is devoted primarily to invertebrates.

As you will see, certain species of fishes are more suitable for the reef tank than are others. However, judicious selection of both invertebrates and fishes, in the course of preparing a plan for stocking the reef tank, can result in your being able to keep a far larger assortment of fish species than is generally recognized.

The first rule of fishkeeping, especially with regard to the reef tank is this: *SET UP A SECOND TANK*!

Whether or not your dealer carries out quarantine procedures (only the better ones do so), it is in your best interests to place newly acquired fishes in a separate tank for a week or two after you bring them home.

This gives you the opportunity to carry out several important procedures. First, you can observe the fish for signs of disease, and treat it appropriately.

Treatments cannot be carried out in the reef tank without serious risk to the invertebrates.

In my experience, medications that purport to be effective against the two most common marine diseases, *Cryptocaryon* (white spot) and *Amblyoodinium* ("oodinium", marine velvet, coral fish disease), and claim to be safe for use in the presence of invertebrates, are of limited value.

Specialized treatments, such as antibiotics, may or may not be safe with the invertebrates you happen to have, and you are taking a grave risk if you introduce these substances into an established reef tank.

While we are on the subject, it is well to point out that most antibiotic preparations that are offered on dealer's shelves carry dosage recommendations that are well below the known therapeutic dose for the antibiotic in question. This is because the manufacturers of these products do not want the medication to wipe out the biological filter in the treatment tank.

However, use of antibiotic treatments at dosages below the therapeutic level causes two problems:

1) you may not be able to cure the disease, and
2) you may simply select for a resistant strain of bacteria that will cause even more problems in the future. If your reef tank is thriving, and water quality is up to par, it is unlikely that your fishes will succumb to infections or parasites.

Nevertheless, any treatment that does become necessary should be done in a tank separate from the main display tank.

Another benefit to be gained from placing new fish

specimens in a separate tank is affording them the opportunity to recover from the stress of capture and shipment.

New specimens should be given the chance to resume normal feeding, and to grow more accustomed to captivity, before they are introduced into a tank full of established fishes. Territorial squabbles, for example, almost certainly will occur, and a recently stressed fish is in a poor position to deal with this situation.

The auxiliary tank need not be an elaborate arrangement. A simple method for establishing a secondary tank follows. Buy a sponge filter and a small air pump. Install the sponge filter in the sump of your trickle filter. Do this about a month before you anticipate the need for an auxiliary tank.

During that period, the sponge will develop a population of nitrifying bacteria. Now you have a portable biological filter that can be transferred to another tank as needed, and will support one or two small fish.

The secondary tank itself can be a 10 or 20 gallon aquarium that normally is stored in the closet or garage. You will also need a heater and thermometer for the secondary tank, and a few short sections of PVC pipe.

The PVC pipe will provide shelter for the fish during its stay in the secondary tank, and should be large enough to allow the fish to get completely inside. Choose pipe sizes according to the sizes of the fish you will be placing in the tank. Plumbing stores, and many aquarium shops, will have lots of PVC scraps lying around, which you can usually obtain free for the asking.

When you want to set up the secondary tank, do the following: fill the tank with water from the main tank, and move in the sponge filter. Install the heater, and adjust the temperature to correspond to that of the main tank. Drop in a couple of PVC pipe sections. Locate the tank in an area that receives moderate light.

It is best not to subject new fish to normal reef tank lighting during the holding period. Ambient room lighting is sufficient to enable you to observe the new specimen.

You can cover the tank to keep the fish from jumping out, but this is only necessary for species that are prone to escape in this fashion (jawfish and eels, for example).

Contrary to popular belief, most fishes will not jump out of the tank, unless startled. When all is in readiness, obtain a new specimen or two.

The process of introducing a fish to a new tank is important. Probably every aquarist is aware that some sort of "acclimation" procedure is necessary, and everyone has a preferred method of doing this.

However, studies that I have conducted with hundreds of marine fishes would indicate that most of the usual methods are really of little benefit, if the intent is to get the fish slowly accustomed to "new" water conditions.

Most acclimation procedures require about an hour's time for the transition. This is simply not a sufficient time for the fish to make the necessary physiological adjustments if water conditions are significantly different. Nevertheless, we should not just open the shipping bag and dump the fish into the tank.

Here are some ideas on moving fish that I have developed over the years.

First, it is important to stop and think about the nature of the journey the fish has made from the dealer's tank to your home. If the dealer is 10 minutes away, obviously the water in the shipping bag will be in better condition than if the journey has lasted several hours.

(If you stopped at the grocery on the way home and left the fish on the seat of your car parked in the sun, shame on you!)

The first thing to do is equalize temperature between the bag and the tank. The important thing to remember here is that an increase in temperature is easier for the fish to deal with than a decrease.

Therefore, if the bag is cooler than the tank, which is the most common situation, you can float the unopened bag in the tank for a half hour or so to allow the temperatures to equalize.

However, if the tank is cooler than the bag, it is better to turn up the thermostat and warm the holding tank to a temperature equal to or greater than that of the bag before proceeding.

Once you have the temperature situation in hand, you can concentrate on the other water parameters. If the fish in the bag appears to be in severe distress, your best bet may be to open the bag and dump the fish into the tank! Presumably, however, the fish will only exhibit mild stress.

Open the bag and drop in an airstone. Adjust the airflow so that a good stream of bubbles is produced, but not so much as to slosh the fish around in the bag (as this will only increase its stress).

The prime enemy in this situation is carbon dioxide.

Carbon dioxide builds up in the shipping water, as a result of the fish's respiration.

If the concentration of CO_2 becomes high enough, the fish will die of respiratory distress, even if there is abundant oxygen present in the water. Aeration of the water in the bag eliminates a lot of CO_2 quickly.

Next, check the water in the bag for ammonia and nitrite. Ammonia will only be present if the fish's journey has been a long one, and nitrite will most likely not be present at all. If ammonia is present, you should get the fish into ammonia-free water as soon as you can.

If nitrite is present, it was probably present in the tank from which the fish was taken. (Checking the shipping water will tell you a lot about the condition of the dealer's tank from which the water was taken. This information will, in turn, be useful in deciding whether to patronize this dealer in the future).

Next, check the pH and specific gravity of the water in the bag. If they are not greatly different from the readings in the tank, you can go ahead and release the fish. If these parameters are significantly different from those in the tank, pour out about half the water in the bag, and add a small amount of water from the tank.

Check pH and specific gravity again. Keep adding tank water every five minutes or so until the pH and specific gravity are equalized, and then release the fish into the tank.

Butterflyfish seem particularly sensitive to sudden pH changes. Most other fishes can be released in the tank once the bag pH is within 0.1 pH units of the tank pH.

Once the fish is in your holding tank, turn out the room

lights and walk away. Leave the new arrival alone for 24 hours, to allow it to become accustomed to its new environment in peace. Offer fresh or frozen food after the first 24 hours. Some fish will start eating promptly; others may take 3-4 days to settle down and start feeding.

Observe the fish carefully for signs of disease: scratching, rapid breathing, sores or lesions, lethargy, etc. After the third day, most fish will be normally active and searching for food.

If disease symptoms are apparent, take appropriate treatment measures. Check pH, ammonia and nitrite in the holding tank, and change water if necessary.

Otherwise, continue feeding for two weeks, and then move the fish to the display tank, using the same acclimation procedures outlined above.

Presumably, conditions in the display tank will be very similar to those in the holding tank, and acclimation will be brief. If you follow these procedures, you should have few problems.

After the holding tank has served its purpose, it should be emptied and the sponge filter soaked in hot, chlorinated tap water for a few hours. The sponge filter can then be returned to the sump of the trickle filter to develop another complement of nitrifying bacteria for future use.

If you plan on introducing fish more frequently than once a month, you may want to use two sponge filters in rotation, so that one will always be biologically active and ready for use in the holding tank.

Storing the tank, heater, and PVC pipe in a dry condition

will insure that parasites and bacteria that may have been present will die. If you have used the holding tank to treat a serious, contagious disease condition, use a solution of household bleach to sterilize everything before re-use.

You can set up a 10 gallon holding tank for about $25, and a 20 gallon system should be less than $50. This is about the price range for one nice fish. Cheap insurance, in my opinion.

Now that we have covered how to handle the fishes that you will be buying for your reef tank, let us turn our attention to the species that will be appropriate. Admit from the start that you cannot keep everything that you might like to have.

Even large dealers face this problem, since tank space is finite, and not all fishes are mutually compatible. I have access to over 5000 gallons of saltwater tanks, yet cannot always have every species I might want. The key to success is proper management of the resources you do have available, and this takes some forethought.

In order to develop a stocking plan for your reef tank's fish population, you of course need some idea of the types of fishes that will be compatible with the invertebrates in the tank. When considering the great diversity of reef fishes, I have found it helpful to use the groupings that biologists employ to categorize fishes.

Related genera of fishes are grouped into families. As a rule of thumb, if a trait is typical of one member of a particular fish family, it is a safe bet that the other members of this family exhibit that same trait, too. All tangs are vegetarians, for example.

Listed below are the families of fishes that are, with a

few exceptions, suitable for the reef aquarium. The scientific names of the families appear in parentheses after the common name:

Squirrel-and soldierfishes (*Holocentridae*)
Trumpetfishes (*Aulostomidae*)
Shrimpfishes (*Centriscidae*)
Pipefishes and Seahorses (*Syngnathidae*)
Lion- and Scorpionfishes (*Scorpaenidae*)
Basslets and Anthias (*Serranidae*)
Dottybacks (*Pseudochromidae*)
Hawkfishes (*Cirrhitidae*)
Cardinalfishes (*Apogonidae*)
Clownfishes and Damselfishes (*Pomacentridae*)
Blennies (*Blenniidae*)
Dragonets (*Callionymidae*)
Jawfishes (*Opistognathidae*)
Dartfishes (*Microdesmidae*)
Gobies (*Gobiidae*)
Tangs (*Acanthuridae*)
Rabbitfishes (*Siganidae*)

In addition, at least some members of two other families can be kept with many invertebrates: the Angelfishes (*Pomacanthidae*) and the Wrasses (*Labridae*).

An important subset of the groups listed are those that will not bother corals, anemones, and other coelenterates, but may feed on shrimps, other crustaceans, and smaller fishes. These include:

Squirrel- and soldierfishes (*Holocentridae*)
Trumpetfishes (*Aulostomidae*)
Lion- and Scorpionfishes (*Scorpaenidae*)
Basslets and Groupers (*Serranidae*)
Dottybacks (*Pseudochromidae*)
Hawkfishes (*Cirrhitidae*)
Cardinalfishes (*Apogonidae*)

A member of any of these families is not to be trusted with any active organism that is small enough to fit into its mouth. Of the groups listed, basslets and anthias, dottybacks, hawkfishes, and cardinalfishes have smaller members that can be kept with most invertebrates.

Examples of fully reef compatible serranids include: Royal Gramma (*Gramma loreto*), Black-capped Basslet (*G. melacara*), Swissguard Basslet (*Liopropoma rubre*), all from the Atlantic, and Squareblock Anthias (*Pseudanthias pleurotaenia*) from the Pacific.

Keep one male anthias with several females, as this is the normal arrangement for anthias in nature. Females are quite different in appearance from the males. In *P. pleurotaenia* the male is pink with a square purple patch on his side, and blue margins on his fins. Females are yellow-orange, with red edging on the scales and red lines running from the mouth to the tail.

In nature, anthias live in open water above reefs in groups in which one male will control a harem of several to many females. Should anything happen to the male, one of the females will change, with amazing rapidity, into a male. If not kept in groups, anthias will often refuse to eat, and will simply cower in a corner of the tank and starve.

Among the dottybacks, Strawberry Dottyback (*Pseudochromis porphyreus*), Bicolor Dottyback (*P. paccagnellae*), Diadema Dottyback (*P. diadema*) are readily available and inexpensive reef tank inhabitants.

Keep only one species per tank, unless the tank is very large. Several beautiful dottybacks come from the Red Sea and the Persian Gulf.

From the former location, the Sunrise Dottyback,

(*Pseudochromis flavivertex*) and the Orchid Dottyback (*P. fridmani*) are the most beautiful. The Neon Dottyback (*P. dutoiti*) comes from the Persian Gulf, and is extraordinarily attractive, with bright orange coloration highlighted by stripes of intense blue. Any of these three fishes, however, may cost upwards of $100.

Two of the hawkfishes are ideally suited for the reef tank. Both have small mouths, and will not prey on your prized cleaner shrimps, etc. These are the Longnosed Hawkfish (*Oxycirrhites typus*) and the Flame Hawkfish (*Neocirrhites armatus*).

The former is colored in a red and white checkerboard pattern, while the latter is bright red with a black stripe on the dorsal fin and a black ring around the eye.

Specimens of some of the many species of cardinalfishs are available from time to time. The most desirable one is *Sphaeramia nematoptera*, usually called the Pajama Cardinal.

Few scorpionfishes can be trusted not to swallow smaller fishes or crustaceans, but no member of this family will harm corals or other coelenterates. In addition, it is well to remember that scorpionfishes (and rabbitfishes, which are vegetarians) bear venomous spines that can cause a painful, and possibly dangerous, sting, if carelessly handled by the aquarist.

Several species of lionfish are available commercially. These differ only in size and color patterns, and all require the same care.

Feed lionfishes every two or three days with frozen or live marine fishes (e.g., lancefish), and other seafoods.

Foods derived from the ocean are of utmost importance

in the diet of lionfishes, which will not live out their normal lifespan if fed exclusively on freshwater fish, such as live goldfish.

Dwarf lionfish (genus *Dendrochirus*) rarely exceed six inches in length. Members of the genus *Pterois*, such as the commonly available *P. volitans*, eventually reach a length of 18 inches or more. Small *Pterois* specimens grow quickly, and can live for 10 years or more in captivity.

If you plan to keep macroalgae in your reef tank, you can rule out all tangs, angelfishes, and rabbitfishes. Algae form the major portion of the diet of these families. If you do not keep macroalgae, however, tangs and rabbitfishes make good additions to the reef tank, and will eliminate microalgae growth, as well.

Angelfishes (*Pomacanthidae*) are a special case. Some are almost exclusively vegetarian, and can be kept with the majority of reef tank invertebrates. Others cannot be trusted not to sample a bit of almost anything they encounter.

None of the larger angelfish species should be attempted, but dwarf angels in the genus *Centropyge* offer some possibilities.

Good choices are the Pygmy Angel (*Centropyge argus*), the only Atlantic species, and several Pacific species, including Potter's Angel (*C. potteri*), Resplendent Angel (*C. resplendens*), Flameback Angel (*C. acanthops*), and the Flame Angel (*C. loriculus*).

Most invertebrates are free from predation by these angelfishes. Notable exceptions are the giant clams and the open brain coral, which are often attacked.

Among the wrasses (*Labridae*), the majority of species are carnivores that may feed on invertebrates such as shrimps, mollusks, worms and echinoderms.

As with the larger angelfishes, large wrasses are not to be trusted in the reef tank. Many smaller wrasses, however, do not pose a threat.

Some widely available "safe" wrasses include the two closely related species commonly called "Neon Wrasse" (*Pseudocheilinus hexataenia* and *P. tetrataenia*), and the social wrasses (genus *Cirrhilabrus*).

If you choose to keep any of the social wrasses (sometimes also called fairy wrasses), make sure you keep them in groups consisting of a single male and several females.

After eliminating those families, in which only certain species can be kept in the reef tank, we are left with the following families in which all members are good reef tank inhabitants:

Shrimpfishes (*Centriscidae*)
Pipefishes and Seahorses (*Syngnathidae*)
Clownfishes and Damselfishes (*Pomacentridae*)
Dragonets (*Callionymidae*)
Blennies (*Blenniidae*)
Jawfishes (*Opistognathidae*)
Dartfishes (*Microdesmidae*)
Gobies (*Gobiidae*)

Shrimpfishes are tiny, and generally spend their lives hanging nose down among the spines of a sea urchin. They require tiny live foods to survive.

A group of shrimpfishes and a large urchin would make a good subject for a small tank devoted to their needs.

Seahorses and pipefishes also require live foods, which means they should be introduced into a reef tank that has been established for a long time, and which thus has developed a population of small crustaceans.

Otherwise, finding a continuous source of the appropriate food may be difficult. Brine shrimp and amphipods are two choices. Many dealers stock live adult brine shrimp, but few have amphipods available.

To culture these live foods at home, you will need considerable space. Newly hatched brine shrimp are too small to be noticed by larger seahorses, so you will need adult brine shrimp.

To rear adult brine shrimp, a large shallow container, such as a child's wading pool, is filled with old tank water and allowed to sit in a brightly lit area until the water turns green, indicating a thriving population of microalgae.

You can add a pinch of houseplant fertilizer to supply nitrate and phosphate for the algae, if your reef tank's water is deficient in these ions (as it should be, but alas, for many people it is not).

Newly hatched brine shrimp are then added. They will feed on the algae and grow to adult size in about three weeks.

Amphipods are the little, transparent shrimp-like creatures that you may have seen scuttling around on the rocks in your tank, feeding on detritus.

You can culture them as follows. Set up a tank with a heater and a large, box-type power filter or a canister filter. Fill the filter compartment with a large sponge block, or polyester filter pads.

You want as much of this material as possible in the
filter, without packing it in so tightly as to restrict water
flow.

Now fill the tank with water containing detritus that you
have siphoned out of your reef tank — the more detritus,
the better. Start the filter running, adjust the heater to
75 degrees, and add a few amphipods that you have
collected from your tank, or from a friend or dealer.

In about a month, the filter material will be teeming with
amphipods, which can easily be harvested by removing
some of the material and swishing it in a bucket of clear
seawater.

Pour this through a net to concentrate the amphipods,
and feed them to your seahorses. Both live adult brine
shrimp and amphipods make an excellent food for small,
reef compatible fishes.

Clownfishes and damselfishes are often the first fishes
that any marine aquarist keeps. They are hardy and
beautiful, and will accept a variety of foods. Most reef
enthusiasts keep clownfishes along with an appropriate
anemone, in order to observe the natural association
between the fish and its coelenterate home.

So much has been written about these fishes that I will
not attempt to summarize it here. Both clowns and
damsels are highly territorial species. Generally, only
one kind of clownfish can be kept in a single tank.

If you try to mix clownfish species in the same aquarium,
at least have a very large tank, and provide extra anemones, at least two per clownfish, or you may have a fight
on your hands.

I once watched in horror as a charming little female

Common Clownfish (*Amphiprion ocellaris*) ripped the fins and gill covers off another female that had inadvertently been introduced into the same tank.

Damselfishes are also known to have a nasty disposition at times. To minimize territorial disputes, keep only one kind of damselfish. If you keep several individuals of the same species together, each fish must be provided with its own cave or niche.

This spot will be vigorously defended by the resident damselfish, even unto death. Damsels are fearless. To illustrate this, I recall a number of visits that I made to the now-closed marine laboratory of the University of Miami, located on tiny Pigeon Key, Florida.

On each visit, I would go snorkeling around the dock, and visit the home of a Beau Gregory Damselfish (*Eupomacentrus leucostictus*) that lived there. (I do not know if it was the same fish every year, but the same hole was always occupied by a Beau Gregory).

Mind you, this beautiful yellow and blue fish is only about an inch long. Invariably, at my approach the fish would swim boldly out of its hole and peck visciously at my face mask, attempting to drive me away, I suppose. Since I am over six feet tall, it is obvious that the fish would not hesitate to tackle fishes much larger than itself.

Perhaps the most popular of the damselfishes is the Blue Devil (*Chrysiptera cyanea*). This fish can be kept in groups in the aquarium, if you pay attention to sex ratios. On the reef it occurs in groups consisting of a single male and several females and juveniles. Overall body color of both sexes is a stunning electric blue.

Females and juveniles have a black spot on the posterior

base of the dorsal fin, and have colorless tail fins. Males lack the black spot, and have bright orange-yellow tails.

This is one of the few damselfish species that display obvious external sexual differences. Incidentally, in the Philippines, the male Blue Devil lacks both the black spot and the orange tail.

Do not confuse the male Blue Devil with the Yellowtail Damsel (*Chromis xanthura*), which is also blue with a yellow tail as a juvenile. In *Chromis*, however, the lobes of the tail fin are sharply pointed, while in *Chrysiptera* they are rounded.

Many species of *Chromis* damsels are imported. If kept in schools, they are an excellent addition to the reef tank. *Chromis* form shoals in open water over reefs, where they feed on plankton.

Only three dragonets are commonly imported for the aquarium. One of these, the Scooter "Blenny" fish (*Synchiropus ocellatus*) is rather drably colored, and is, unfortunately, almost always imported from the Philippines.

For various reasons, including offshore pollution and the use of cyanide and other drugs in collecting, Philippine fishes may do poorly in captivity, despite the best efforts of the aquarist. This situation is changing, however, as efforts to institute wiser fishery management in the Philippines are beginning to take effect.

S. ocellatus is far outshone in beauty by two related species. Both are bottom dwelling fishes, with docile habits and exquisite coloration.

The Mandarin (*Synchiropus splendidus*) and the Spotted Mandarin (*S. picturatus*) are ideal specimens for the reef tank. In all dragonets, the male can be distinguished from the female by the greatly elongated first spine of the dorsal fin, and his larger size.

You can keep mandarins of the same species together as trios consisting of one male and two females, and you can keep the two mandarin species together, but never, ever put two male mandarins of the same species together in the tank. They will fight until one is killed.

Mandarins are seldom bothered by other fishes, perhaps because they are poisonous if eaten. The gaudy coloration and non-secretive habits of the fish lend credence to this supposition.

There are lots and lots of blennies, and they have much to recommend them as aquarium fish. For one thing, combtooth blennies, typified by the Red-Lipped Blenny (*Ophioblennius atlanticus*) from Florida, the Bicolor Blenny (*Escenius bicolor*) from Indonesia and Australia, and the wide-ranging Midas Blenny (*E. midas*), feed largely on microalgae.

Either species will even eat "red slime" algae, which many other fishes dislike. The Midas Blenny is ochre in color with a blue belly. The Bicolor Blenny is usually dark brown with an orange abdomen and tail, and the Red-Lipped Blenny is brown, with distinctive bright red lips.

"Eyelash" blennies (genus *Cirrhipectes*) are also members of the combtooth blenny tribe, and also help to rid the aquarium of microalgae. These blennies can be recognized by their cirri, the "eyelashes". Several species appear in shipments.

The saber-toothed blennies do not feed upon algae, but rather upon small bottom-dwelling crustaceans. They swim actively in the open water, largely free from fear of predators, because they all have poisonous fangs! Any fish foolish enough to grab one of these blennies will have the inside of its mouth painfully bitten repeatedly, and will usually spit out the feisty "meal".

This trait is used only in defense, however, and the blenny will not bite other fish unless harassed. Saber-toothed blennies of the genus *Meiacanthus* are also called lyretail blennies, because of the shape of the tail.

The two lyretail blennies most often available to aquarists are actually subspecies of the same species, *M. atrodorsalis*, that differ strikingly in coloration. The Canary Blenny, *M. atrodorsalis ovaluensis*, is bright yellow and is found only around the Fiji Islands.

The more wide-ranging *M. artrodorsalis atrodorsalis*, is baby blue with a pale green tail and has a black line running through the middle of the dorsal fin and continuing through the center of the eye.

It is given a variety of common names in the aquarium trade, including the especially confusing name "Eyelash Blenny."

Probably because of their poisonous fangs, the color patterns of many of the saber-toothed blennies are mimicked by other fishes, which thereby also gain protection from predators.

Another case of mimicry in blennies is well-known, and involves two undesirable members of the saber-tooth blenny clan :

- *Plagiotremus rhynorhynchus* and
- *Aspidontus taeniatus*

both mimic not only the coloration but also the movements of the cleaner wrasse, *Labroides dimidiatus*.

When an unsuspecting fish approaches one of these masqueraders expecting to be cleaned of parasites, the blenny instead takes a bite from its unfortunate victim.

These blennies feed largely, but not exclusively, upon the bits of fish flesh they obtain in this nefarious manner. Ironically, *P. taeniatus* has actually been observed receiving the services of the cleaner wrasse that it mimics.

Jawfishes are included here largely because I could not decide exactly where to list them. They are thought to be related to the basslets, but their classification is still being debated.

They are excellent aquarium fishes, although inclined to be jumpers. There are some jawfishes that grow much too large to be included in a tank with invertebrates such as shrimps, but these are rarely available, owing to their drab coloration or large size, or both.

New species are being discovered all the time, but, again, they are rarely imported. They require a deep layer of sand in the tank in which to dig their characteristic burrows, and this requirement is at odds with the idea that a reef tank should not have a deep layer of substrate.

Further, they cannot be kept with large anemones, or other stinging coelenterates, because these will eventually catch and eat the jawfish. So why do I include them here? Simple. I like jawfishes. In fact, they are absolutely, positively my favorite aquarium fish.

There is simply nothing so charming as a group of jawfishes each hovering just above its vertical burrow, large, expressive eyes alert to every movement. Each fish builds itself a pile of shells and gravel at the entrance to the burrow, and each spends quite a bit of time raiding the pile belonging to its neighbor. Try as I may,

I cannot discern why a particular shell or rock might be so desirable, except maybe for the simple fact that it was stolen; in days gone by, a cookie purloined from the plate when Mom was not looking always tasted better somehow. Perhaps it is the same with jawfish and pebbles.

Two species of jawfish are collected for the aquarium. One of these, the Blue Spotted Jawfish (*Opistognathus* sp.), from the Sea of Cortez, is infrequently seen and usually expensive. Far more common is the Yellow-headed Jawfish (*O. aurifrons*) from Florida and the Caribbean.

Yellowheaded Jawfish can be kept singly or in groups (a group is more fun to watch) in any size aquarium that will accommodate the number of fishes you want to keep. They must be provided with sand, gravel, crushed shells or a mixture of these, in which they will excavate vertical burrows.

They feed on planktonic organisms snatched from the water column, and thus are easy to feed in the aquarium, accepting a variety of fresh and/or frozen foods, such as adult brine shrimp, mysis shrimp, bloodworms and blackworms.

Jawfish are mouthbrooders, with the male carrying the eggs until they hatch, and they have spawned in captivity. If you want to try a few jawfish in your reef tank, it can probably be done, if you can arrange to create an area of substrate on the otherwise bare bottom of the tank.

Do not be overly concerned about accumulation of detritus or anaerobic areas in this substrate material, as the excavations of the jawfish will keep it amply stirred up.

Finally we come to the gobies, a group of fishes comprising several families, and the group with the greatest number of species in tropical seas.

Many new gobies are discovered every year. Virtually all gobies are peaceful, small fishes that feed on small benthic or planktonic invertebrates. They are thus all suitable fishes for the reef tank.

Rather than attempt to describe the vast number of gobies that one might find in the well-stocked aquarium shop, I will mention one or two representatives of each of the groups into which the goby clan is divided.

Ichthyologists have grouped fishes generally called gobies into two families, but for aquarium purposes, we will consider five groups.

Family *Microdesmidae*, the dartfishes, includes two aquarium groups, fire gobies and torpedo gobies. Certainly the most familiar of these are the fire gobies. The Firefish (*Nemateleotris magnifica*) is found in several locations in the Indo-Pacific region.

It has a cream colored body, with a brilliant flame red tail, and hovers in midwater with its elongated dorsal fin held erect. Juvenile Firefish are sometimes found in small groups, but only one Firefish can be kept in the aquarium, unless you are lucky enough to find a mated pair.

Among the torpedo gobies, the Blue Gudgeon (*Ptereleotris heteroptera*) is typical. It is an elongated species, shaped, in other words, like a torpedo, and is solid baby blue with a single black splotch in the fork of the tail.

This species will spend more time out in the open if kept in a group. They do not squabble among themselves, as is the case with the Firefish. The Blue Gudgeon is a good jumper, unfortunately.

Among the Gobiidae, or true gobies, are three groups, for aquarium purposes. These are the partner gobies, the signal gobies, and all others. I'll mention a couple of species in the "all others" category first, and then discuss the weird signal goby, and the fascinating partner gobies.

The Neon Goby (*Gobiosoma oceanops*) was among the first marine fishes to be spawned in captivity, and today thousands of them are hatchery produced. Just over an inch in length, black in color with brilliant blue and white horizontal stripes, the Neon Goby is at home in any reef tank.

Pairs can be obtained by keeping a group of juveniles together and allowing them to pair off as they grow. This species is also a cleaner. As you can see, there is much to recommend the Neon Goby to any aquarist.

Much larger than the Neon Goby, the six inch Golden Headed Sleeper Goby (*Valenciennea strigata*) lives in pairs in a cave that is constructed by the fish under a rock or other structure. Males are distinguished from females by the long filaments extending upward from the anterior end of the dorsal fin.

These gobies (as well as several other *Valenciennea* species that are imported from time to time) like to dig in the sand, "chewing" the grains to obtain small crustaceans and worms upon which they feed.

They will keep the substrate stirred up nicely, if you are a reef keeper who likes a thin layer of sand on the bottom of the tank. Interestingly, these gobies are known to communicate with each other via signals produced by the mouth. Since ichthyologists have reclassified this group, *Valenciennea* is no longer technically a "sleeper" goby (Family *Eleotridae*).

Perhaps a suitable new common name would be "Golden Headed Talking Goby", in honor of their communication capabilities.

Signal gobies, which are closely related to *Valenciennea*, may also signal to each other with their mouths, but that is not where the common name comes from. The huge eyespots on the dorsal fins inspired the name Signal Goby for the single species *Signigobius biocellatus*.

This goby mimics, of all things, a crab. When threatened, the goby extends the dorsal fins to display the eyespots, which, together with the dark blue pectoral and pelvic fins, is intended to give the impression of a large, aggressive crab, to deter predators. The goby even mimics the sideways movement of a crab.

On the reef, *Signigobius* is found exclusively in mated pairs, and should only be kept as such in the aquarium. Deprived of its mate, a solitary individual will soon die, apparently of loneliness, a cruel fate that should not be imposed by an uninformed aquarist.

These gobies "chew" the substrate to obtain food, but will also take food from midwater. If you can obtain a pair, and they are often imported from Australia, the Signal Goby makes a fine addition to the reef tank.

The last group of gobies represents, for me at least, one of the most remarkable adaptations to be found in the sea. These are the partner gobies, of which there are several species.

I will describe only one, the Blue-Spotted Yellow Watchman Goby (*Cryptocentrus cinctus*), which, true to its name is yellow in color with blue dots all over the body.

Watchman gobies all have large eyes that are located high on the head. The coloration and appearance of this goby is enough to make it attractive to the aquarist, but the relationship that these gobies have with certain species of *alpheid* shrimps is truly amazing.

Partner gobies live in areas of loose rubble, sand and gravel, but are unable to dig a burrow into which they can escape from predators. That duty is carried out by the partner shrimp, which has specially modified claws for digging.

A shrimp and a pair of gobies may share the same burrow, or only a single goby may occupy the burrow, but the shrimp is always present. The goby feeds on small organisms exposed by the excavations of the shrimp.

So what does the poor, hardworking shrimp get from the association? A pair of eyes. The shrimp is nearly blind, and thus cannot see the approach of a predator. When the goby leaves the burrow, the shrimp trails behind, always keeping one of its antennae in contact with its roommate. If danger threatens, the goby flicks its tail to warn the shrimp, and both dart back to the safety of the burrow.

The association must be of great benefit both to shrimp and goby, since over 25 species of partner gobies and at least 8 species of associated shrimps are known.

If you wish to obtain a partner goby and shrimp, always make sure the association is established in the aquarium before you buy. Some of these associations are very specific, not just any shrimp/goby pair will take up with each other. Also, do not buy the goby without the shrimp.

Unable to dig, and faced with the lack of a burrow, the goby may very well refuse to eat and thus slowly starve in the aquarium.

This brief overview of fishes for the reef tank should be supplemented with readings from several of the excellent books on marine fishes that are now available.

Two that have been especially useful to me are :

• *Fishes for the Invertebrate Aquarium,* by Helmut Debelius, published by Aquarium Systems, and
• *Micronesian Reef Fishes*, by Robert F. Meyers, published by Coral Graphics.

Both books should be available from your dealer, along with a host of other titles.

A. Thiel's *Advanced Reef Keeping II, The Invertebrates* was not out at the time of this writing and could not be evaluated. Based on personal conversations with Albert this should prove to be one of the most interesting books to come out in the near future.

Chapter Fourteen

Nutrition in the Reef Tank

Reef tank invertebrates require certain elements in order to grow and reproduce in the normal manner. We have already seen, in Chapter Eleven, that iron is of critical importance to the maintenance of macroalgae.

Other elements that are important to reef invertebrates include calcium, strontium, molybdenum, and iodine.

Let us examine the role that each of these plays in the aquarium, and discuss how the aquarist can be certain that proper levels of these elements are maintained.

• **Calcium.**

Natural seawater contains approximately 412 mg/l of calcium. This chemical element is required by all forms of life, but is especially important to organisms than secrete a calcium carbonate skeleton, or in which a component of the exoskeleton is calcium carbonate.

These organisms include certain macroalgae, corals, certain mollusks and tubeworms, crustaceans, and echinoderms. Clearly, the importance of calcium to the reef tank cannot be overestimated. All of the organisms mentioned above extract calcium from the water. This can lead to a depletion of calcium from the tank.

The body processes of the calcium-extracting organisms are adapted to operate at the calcium concentration found in natural seawater; it should therefore be obvious that allowing levels of calcium in the reef tank to fall below about 400 mg/l can be detrimental to these organisms.

Thus, it is prudent to add a calcium supplement to the tank on a regular basis. Many articles that emphasize this fact have appeared recently in hobbyist magazines.

Testing for calcium is relatively easy. Calcium hardness test kits are available that measure the concentration of calcium carbonate in water in parts per million. (For all practical purposes, this is equivalent to mg/l $CaCO_3$.)

The calcium concentration of the water can be calculated from the calcium carbonate concentration simply by multiplying by 0.4. Thus, the ideal concentration of calcium carbonate for the reef tank would be about 1000 parts per million (1000 ppm $CaCO_3$ X 0.4 = 400 ppm Ca).

Various supplements are available to supply calcium to the reef tank. These are solutions of either calcium hydroxide [$Ca(OH)_2$] or calcium chloride ($CaCl_2$).

A saturated solution of calcium hydroxide is most commonly used in Europe, and is called kalkwasser. In the United States, *Kalkwasser* is manufactured by Thiel-Aqua-Tech Inc. of Las Cruces, New Mexico.

Alternatively, you can prepare your own solution using 3 grams of calcium hydroxide to one liter of distilled water. Mix the powder with the water in a suitable container. Cap the container, entrapping as little air as possible, and mix thoroughly. *CAUTION! THE REACTION PRODUCES HEAT.*

Allow to stand overnight, and decant the clear liquid. Some of the powder will settle to the bottom, and can be reused to make another batch. Exercise extreme caution with both the dry powder and the prepared solution. Both are caustic.

The solution (which, by the way, is called "limewater", in this country) will have a pH of about 12. Therefore, it must be added to the aquarium in very small amounts, lest you increase the pH of the tank above desirable levels.

A solution of calcium chloride will not alter the pH of the aquarium, but must be used along with a calcium test kit to insure that calcium levels in the aquarium are not elevated too much.

Five grams of calcium chloride ($CaCl_2$), dissolved in one liter of water yields a solution with a concentration of 5 mg calcium chloride per ml (5 mg/ml). Now, how much calcium is in 5 mg of calcium chloride?

To answer this, we need to calculate the percent by weight of calcium in calcium chloride. The atomic weight of calcium is 40, the atomic weight of chlorine is 35, and there are two chlorine atoms per molecule of calcium chloride. Thus, 40 + 35 + 35 equals 110, the molecular weight of calcium chloride.

Therefore, for a given amount of calcium chloride, the weight of the calcium only will be 40/110, or 36 percent of the total. Thirty-six percent of 5 mg is 1.8 mg (0.36 X 5 = 1.8).

Thus, each ml of the solution in this example will contain 1.8 mg of calcium, and say 0.15 ml would contain 0.27 mg of calcium, for example.

Let us s consider another example, to show you how these chemistry calculations can be carried out to gain useful information.

In the Summer 1990 issue of Seascope, published by Aquarium Systems, a table is presented that shows the concentrations of various elements found in various brands of synthetic seawater mixes.

The phosphorous concentration for Instant Ocean is given as 0.19 mg/l. How much phosphate is that? (One might want to know this because test kits usually measure phosphate, not phosphorous itself.) To find the answer, we first must calculate the molecular weight of phosphate, PO_4. The atomic weight of phosphorous is 31, and the atomic weight of oxygen is 16.

We can see from the formula that four atoms of oxygen are present in each phosphate molecule. Therefore, the molecular weight of phosphate is 31 + 16 + 16 + 16 + 16, or 95. The percent by weight of phosphorous in phosphate is thus 31/95 or 33 percent. To find the amount of phosphate represented by 0.19 mg of phosphorus, we divide by 0.33. Our answer is 0.19/.33 = 0.58, or about 0.6 mg/l phosphate for this seawater mix.

With a table of atomic weights, and the chemical formula of the compound in which you are interested, you can calculate the weight percent of any element you wish. This can be most helpful if you are attempting to formulate your own water additives, for example.

I would caution you, however, to double check your calculations, or review them with a more experienced aquarist, before you hasten to create "home brewed" tank additives and dump them into your tank.

A mistake can be much more costly, in terms of replacing animals killed by improper formulations, than simply buying the additive off the shelf at your local dealer.

While on the subject of do-it-yourself additives, I have noted a significant increase in telephone calls from aquarists wanting to find sources for various chemicals, calcium hydroxide for making limewater, strontium chloride for preparing strontium supplement, potassium iodide for preparing iodine supplement, etc.

Most of the large chemical supply houses with which I am familiar are very reluctant to make sales of chemicals to individuals, because of the liabilities involved. However, most cities of reasonable size (say 200,000 people or more) have industrial or manufacturing chemists from whom chemicals can be obtained or ordered.

Pharmacists are sometimes willing to order chemical compounds, provided you explain what they are to be used for. Another potential source is your local high school chemistry teacher, who may be able to help you order the compounds you need.

None of these sources, however, is likely to sell chemicals to a person who obviously exhibits little knowledge of the chemical's properties (toxic, caustic, etc.) or who does not seem to know exactly how to use the chemical safely and wisely.

Educate yourself on these matters before you attempt to purchase any chemicals.

Calcium hydroxide used in making limewater, for example, is extremely caustic and can burn your skin or eyes. I can only repeat what I said earlier: Make sure you understand the basic chemistry involved in preparing your own tank supplements; otherwise, you may be better off to buy ready made products, despite the added cost.

If you are ready to learn the chemistry involved, however, I can suggest two very valuable sources of information. One is a good college chemistry textbook. Keenan and Wood's *Modern College Chemistry* is a good bet.

I had the opportunity to benefit from Dr. Keenan's expertise, both as chemist and as teacher, when I was a freshman at the University of Tennessee, where he is a professor of chemistry.

The other is *The Merck Index*, published by Merck and Co., Rahway, NJ. This book should be in your local library. This encyclopedia of chemicals, drugs and biological products lists, alphabetically, virtually every chemical compound in industrial use, and give valuable data about each compound.

For example, the entry for calcium hydroxide reads, in part, as follows:
"Calcium Hydroxide. Calcium hydrate; slaked lime. $Ca(OH)2$; mol wt. 74.10....Crystals or soft, odorless granules or powder. Slightly bitter, alkaline taste. ... Slightly sol[uble] in water..." The Merck Index gives this sort of information, and more, for 10,000 chemical compounds.

From the earlier example, it should be apparent that, in order to increase significantly the concentration of calcium in an aquarium by using calcium chloride, one needs quite a bit of the chemical.

Generally speaking, it is better to use calcium chloride in dry form to increase the calcium concentration by a large amount, and then use limewater solution (calcium hydroxide), in small amounts, as an aid in maintaining the calcium concentration of the tank.

Let's do one more calculation, this time to determine how much dry calcium chloride is needed to raise the calcium concentration of a 20 gallon tank from 200 mg/l to 400 mg/l.

First, calculate how many milligrams of calcium ion are needed. Twenty gallons is about 80 liters, and we want to increase the concentration by 200 mg/l. Thus, 80 X 200 = 16,000 mg, or 16 grams of calcium. For dry calcium chloride, 36% by weight is calcium. Thus, 16 grams divided by 0.36 is 44.4 grams of calcium chloride.

It is important to mention that we have done this calculation with material that is chemically dry or anhydrous.

Calcium chloride is usually available as a hydrated form. Each molecule of $CaCl_2$ is accompanied by several molecules of water, called "water of hydration".

Often, six molecules of water are present, and the material is called "calcium chloride hexahydrate". We must account for the water in our calculations.

To the molecular weight of calcium chloride itself, we add the molecular weight of 6 molecules of water, 108, to find the total weight of 218.

Calcium itself thus represents only 18% of the total weight of the hydrated form (40/218 = .18). Thus, if we used the hexahydrate form of calcium chloride in the example above, we will need 88.9 grams to provide 16 grams of calcium ion for the 20 gallon tank.

• **Strontium**.

Strontium is present in natural seawater at a concentration of 7.9 mg/l.

There is no simple, commercially available test kit for strontium, but many European aquarists use a supplement containing 10% strontium chloride (SrCl2) in distilled water at the rate of 1.0 ml per 150 liters of aquarium water on a weekly basis.

Charles Delbeek and Julian Sprung, writing in hobbyist magazines, have produced several excellent articles on the subject of inorganic supplements for reef tanks. Serious reef enthusiasts should seek out back issues, as well as keeping alert for future works by either of these two fine authors. I am much indebted to both of them for much valuable information that has formed the background for this book.

Commercially prepared supplements containing strontium are available e.g. from Coralife and Thiel Aqua Tech (KSM), as well as from other sources.

• **Molybdenum**.

Molybdenum is required by corals because it is involved in the process whereby the coral secretes its skeleton. The concentration of molybdenum in natural seawater is 10 micrograms per liter (10 parts per billion, approximately).

Thus, it is not practical to test for molybdenum, and only a very tiny amount is needed.

Commercially available supplements advertised to contain molybdenum as well as strontium include "KSM" Supplement, by Thiel-Aqua-Tech, and "Strontium Plus" by Coralife. Other "trace element" supplements may contain this element, but I am unable to say for sure, as most manufacturers do not list the contents of their products on the label. (A lamentable practice, that ideally will change in the future.)

Good quality synthetic seawater mixes also contain molybdenum, usually at a concentration several times that of natural seawater. If you are performing water changes on a regular basis, it is likely that this element is abundantly available in your tank.

• Iodine.

Iodine is present in natural seawater at a concentration of 60 micrograms per liter (60 parts per billion).

This element is essential to all organisms, but is especially necessary for macroalgae, soft corals, and crustaceans. If shrimps die during the process of molting, you should suspect a deficientcy of iodine in the aquarium water.

Some aquarists use a solution of potassium iodide to supplement the tank, because this element is depleted by the use of ozone and protein skimmers, as well as by absorption by living organisms.

Unless you thoroughly understand the chemistry involved, I do not advocate preparing your own iodine supplement, as overuse of iodine can be extremely harmful to the tank's inhabitants.

Commercially prepared iodine supplements are available from Thiel-Aqua-Tech and Coralife. Again, there may be other products on the market that contain iodine in an appropriate concentration for the aquarium.

Many other trace elements are present in natural sea-water, and a variety of these are known to be required by one or more kinds of marine life.

A number of trace element supplements are available that can be added to the tank to replenish those elements that are depleted from the water by biological processes and aquarium filtration.

I caution the aquarist, however, to resist the temptation to assume that because a supplement is in use that all is well. NONE of the various additives available for use in the reef tank is a suitable substitute for water changes, testing, and good maintenance.

Of all the factors that occupy the interest of reef aquarists in the course of caring for their tanks, perhaps none is given less attention than the quality of the diet of the fishes.

In a well-established reef tank, there will be an abundance of small organisms, microcrustaceans and algae, for example, that serve as food for the fish. While these foods are perhaps the best kind of nourishment for captive fishes, they cannot be relied upon to support a reasonably large fish population indefinitely.

In other words, the fish will need to be fed, albeit infrequently, in any reef tank. The quantity of food given is important, but equally important is the quality of the food, from a nutritional standpoint.

Authors differ in opinions on the subject of feeding the fish in a reef tank. Certainly, one does not feed as often, nor in such quantity, as do the owners of fish-only tanks.

This is in part because of the availability of food organisms within the reef tank, such organisms being notably absent from most fish-only tanks. Another reason is the importance of keeping reef tank water nutrient-poor.

Added foods are a major source of nitrate, phosphate, and dissolved organic carbon, and the concentration of these substances in the water must be kept to a minimum. A large proportion of these nutrient ions will find their way into the water from foods whether eaten or not, by the way.

Nevertheless, the food supply should be adjusted so that as much of the food as possible is consumed by the fishes, rather than being allowed to sink to the bottom and decay. Deciding how much to give at a feeding will take some experimentation on the part of the aquarist, as each community of fishes is different.

As a starting point, add about half as much food as you think the fishes will eat, and then observe the tank after 20 minutes to determine if uneaten food remains. Adjust the quantity given at the next feeding appropriately.

Never mind that the fishes always seem hungry when you approach the tank. Most fishes will eat whenever food is available, unless they have only recently eaten their fill. The fact that they are willing to eat does not mean that they should be fed.

Establish a regular feeding schedule and stick to it. Two or three feedings a week is sufficient. If you desire to feed more frequently than this, if for no other reason than the fun of watching them eat, feed very small amounts.

In point of fact, most reef fishes nibble bits of this and that throughout their waking hours in nature. However, few aquarists seem able to develop the restraint necessary to duplicate this situation in the aquarium without adding unnecessary levels of pollution to the water, in the form of uneaten food.

As stated above, what to feed is as important as how much to feed. The general rule here is: feed as wide a variety of foods as possible. Fishes need a balanced diet for all of the same reasons that you do.

You may adore rib eye steak, or ice cream, or broccoli, for that matter, but an exclusive diet of any of these foods would lead to malnutrition eventually, as any doctor can confirm.

There is a huge variety of foods available at any aquarium shop. Make use of this abundance.

Fresh, living foods are preferable to any sort of prepared foods. However, convenience will dictate that prepared foods will have to be used, at least part of the time. With marine fishes, it is also important that the bulk of the diet come from marine sources whenever possible, for reasons that will be explained below.

Here are some suggestions from each of the types of foods that are usually available in well-stocked aquarium shops.

• Live foods.

Adult brine shrimp, newly hatched brine shrimp, amphipods, California blackworms, guppies, and baitfish are commonly available.

Each of these foods can be used where appropriate, and each differs in terms of convenience and cost. Any of these live foods should be used, however, for fishes that will eat them.

Do not make the mistake, however, of feeding predatory marine fishes exclusively on guppies or baitfish, or similar type live foods.

See below for an explanation of the problem with this feeding regimen.

• **Fresh foods**.

Few aquarium shops stock fresh foods, because of the short shelf life of these products. However, your grocery stocks an abundance of foods that can be used in the aquarium.

Fresh fish fillets, shrimp, clams, scallops, mussels, and squid can be chopped into pieces appropriate for feeding aquarium fishes. If you prepare these foods for your own consumption, save a bit of fresh food for the fishes in the course of making dinner.

Ocean fish, such as snapper, tuna, mahi-mahi, halibut, sole, cod, and the like, are better foods for marine fishes than are freshwater fishes such as trout and catfish.

The produce department stocks a host of vegetables that are good for herbivorous marine fish. Romaine and other types of lettuce, spinach, parsley, peas, broccoli, and zucchini have all been used with success.

If the fish are finicky about eating these foods initially, blanch them briefly in boiling water before feeding. This will make their consistency more like that of the algae that herbivorous fishes are accustomed to eating.

Wash grocery store vegetables well, to remove any traces of pesticides that may be present, or purchase organically grown produce, if it is available to you.

• Frozen foods.

A host of frozen foods are sold for aquarium use. These range from frozen marine life such as brine shrimp, squid, mysid shrimps, and lancefish, to preparations containing a variety of ingredients and additives.

Brands include Coralife, Ocean Nutrition, Gamma, Lifeline, California Aquatic Foods, San Francisco Bay Brand, Pro-Salt, Kordon, Thiel Aqua Tech, and many others.

Ocean Nutrition even makes a food containing sponges, an important constituent the diet of marine angelfish. Some of these foods (certain Coralife products, for example) are made specifically for reef tanks, with larger chunks for the fishes and smaller particles for filter feeding invertebrates.

In my experience, these are excellent foods. Manufacturers often supply the foods in cube packs, which is very convenient. Frozen foods are probably the best substitute for fresh foods, and come in a much wider variety.

Of course, frozen foods are always available, whereas fresh or live foods may not be. Keep a variety of frozen foods on hand and feed them to your fishes regularly.

• Freeze-dried foods.

Freeze drying preserves almost as much nutritional value as freezing, although certain vitamins may be lost in the process.

Most freeze dried aquarium foods contain crustaceans, such as krill or brine shrimp.

These foods are high in protein and are very convenient,

but should not form the staple diet for marine fish. Use them as a supplement to other foods, to provide variety.

• **Dehydrated and flake foods**.

Dehydration has been used to preserve foods for centuries. While many essential nutrients are lost or destroyed in the dehydration process, dried foods are still nutritious. Moreover, they are cheap and convenient, and certain to be stocked by any aquarium shop. Include these foods as part of a balanced diet for your marine fishes. Choose flake foods that are specifically made for marine fishes.

Reputable manufacturers include ingredients that supply nutrients essential to the fishes for which the food was formulated. Thus, it is wise to stick with major national brands.

Despite the cost savings that accrue when flake foods are bought in quantity, it is best to purchase only a small amount at any one time. After opening, flake foods may lose food value, or worse, develop mold or bacterial growth.

Dried seaweed is seldom sold in aquarium shops, but can be found in Oriental food stores, or in the specialty section of the grocery. Look for nori, a seaweed that is used in making sushi.

It comes in sheets and shreds, and consists only of dried macroalgae. Vegetarian fishes love this product, and it is a more natural food for them than garden vegetables.

Other species of seaweeds are eaten in the Orient, and these will be offered in dried form, as well. Konbu and wakame are two that I have tried, both for my fish and on my plate.

My angelfish didn't seem to like them, although I did, well enough.

These and other seaweeds should be offered to tangs, angelfishes, rabbitfishes, and certain damselfishes and blennies.

• **Food additives**.

With growing awareness on the part of aquarists that certain nutrients are essential for the long-term health of marine fishes, and that often these nutrients are lacking from commercial fish foods, a new category of products for the marine hobbyist has made its appearance on dealer's shelves.

These are food additives, designed to replace important nutrients that some fish foods lack. Vita-Boost, a product of Ocean Nutrition, and Vita-Chem, from Dick Boyd Enterprises, both claim to provide Vitamin C.

The vitamin is supplied in esterified ("stabilized") form, thereby increasing the shelf life of the product. Vita-Boost is used regularly at my store, but I have not yet tried Vita-Chem. Dick Boyd's products have a good reputation, however. See below for more about Vitamin C.

Selcon™ is a new product advertised to contain essential fatty acids along with vitamins C and B-12. Certain fatty acids are recognized to be vitally important in the nutrition of marine fishes.

We will have more to say about fatty acids below. Selcon™ is indeed a useful food additive.

Some general recommendations about handling aquarium foods are in order. Frozen foods should be treated like frozen foods for human consumption. Keep the foods frozen until feeding time, thaw out only what you really need, and do not re-freeze completely thawed food (just as you do with human consumption foods).

All foods should be purchased in small quantities that will be used within a reasonable period of time (one month, or less), and should be stored in the freezer or refrigerator to facilitate maximum retention of nutritional value.

The same goes for food additives. Keep all foods tightly sealed, as oxygen from the air can break down valuable vitamins, and moisture intrusion can lead to spoilage.

Spoiled foods can be recognized by a foul odor; mold growth usually produces a "musty" smell. Discard spoiled or moldy foods immediately. Do not remove the spoiled parts and try to use the balance of the food.

Many aquarists are concerned about transmitting disease to their fishes via fresh or frozen seafoods. This is extremely unlikely. Often in nature sick or injured fishes are eaten by other fishes with no ill effects.

Disease outbreaks in the aquarium can usually be traced to less than optimal water quality, or other conditions that create stress for the fishes and leave them more susceptible to infection. Feeding a wholesome, balanced diet is one way to prevent disease outbreaks.

Most of the foregoing is common sense knowledge. We are all taught the importance of clean, fresh, wholesome food in maintaining our own health — television advertisements touting the importance of fiber, unsaturated fats, vitamins, etc., bombard us daily.

Many people have the notion that fishes are "different" somehow, in regard to foods and nutrition.

Certainly some species have specialized dietary requirements, but the majority of fishes eat a variety of foods. Of course, on the reef all foods are fresh, whether algae or coral polyps are on the menu.

So, pay attention to your fishes' diet. Do not feed the same foodstuffs indiscriminately to all fishes.

Good foods are cheaper, and are much more widely available, than some of the equipment used for setting up a reef tank.

In order to demonstrate the importance of nutrition in maintaining marine fishes in captivity, I shall provide just two examples of common nutritional problems that can be easily avoided.

"Lateral line disease" has long been known to affect captive marine fishes, and has even been reported in wild fishes. This condition is characterized by erosion of the skin tissue along the lateral line and around the face, and is seen especially in tangs and angelfishes.

Until the cause of the problem was elucidated, a variety of remedies were tried, all to no avail, based upon the mistaken assumption that the condition was due to bacterial infection brought on by poor water quality. Recent research has shown that lateral line disease, now more correctly called "lateral line syndrome" is a result of Vitamin C deficiency.

Prevention and cure simply involve feeding your fishes a diet rich in this very important vitamin.

One of the biologists on the staff of my company believes that in some cases a low-grade bacterial infection may accompany lateral line syndrome, and that this infection should be treated with antibiotics along with an improvement in diet. We are currently investigating this aspect of the condition.

Lowered resistance to infection can accompany this form of malnutrition, which may explain why antibiotics sometimes help. Little doubt remains that Vitamin C deficiency is at the root of the syndrome, however.

Prevent lateral line syndrome by feeding fishes fresh foods that are high in Vitamin C, and adding supplements that contain this vitamin to frozen and dried foods.

Vitamin C is notoriously difficult to preserve by traditional storage methods, hence the need for fresh foods and/or supplements.

Green vegetables, such as spinach, and citrus fruits, are good sources of Vitamin C. If you are skeptical about feeding citrus fruits to angelfishes, I suggest you try it some time.

Fatty acid deficiency is a slow and insidious form of malnutrition that can affect large, predatory fishes such as lionfishes and groupers. The marine fish that form the bulk of the diet of these species are rich in highly unsaturated fatty acids.

These compounds are essential to the health of many aquarium fishes. Feeding lionfishes exclusively on baitfish, a common practice, condemns the lionfish to an early death. I have conducted necropsies (dissections) on many lionfish in which the liver showed obvious signs of fatty acid deficiency.

To avoid the problem, feed ocean-derived foods, including fish, and use a supplement such as Selcon™, mentioned above.

Cod liver oil has also been used successfully to provide essential fatty acids in the diet of captive marine fish.

While the nature of the dietary problem has not yet been identified, there is another example of malnutrition in aquarium fish that I would like to report.

The species most commonly affected are puffers, porcupine fish, and spiny boxfish. None of these species is suitable for the reef tank. I mention them here as an illustration of how improper diet can lead to trouble.

I have seen a number of cases in which one of these fish lost the ability to eat, specifically the ability to move its jaws, and one case in which the fish lost all its teeth. In every case, the fish had been fed freeze-dried krill exclusively for several months before the problem developed. Now, this is not evidence that krill is bad for fish. It is evidence, however, that an unbalanced diet can lead to problems.

In nature, fishes such as these feed on a wide variety of invertebrates and smaller fishes. It is not surprising that they would suffer problems from a diet consisting of a single food. Never mind that the fish eat krill quite readily. I do the same with ice cream, but would not recommend an exclusive diet of ice cream for anyone.

In each of these cases the fish eventually died of starvation, or became so debilitated that they were euthanized. Sad, for species that can live to be ten years old or more in captivity. This illustration leads me to ask how many other problems, in particular those with no obvious "cause", that have been observed in aquarium fish could have been traced to improper or inadequate diet. Better to be safe than sorry. Feed your marine fishes the widest possible variety of foods, and make sure those foods are of the highest quality you can obtain.

Chapter Fifteen

Recent Trends in Reefkeeping

Since this book was completed, two important trends have begun to develop among American reef hobbyists.

One is a dawning recognition of the need to eliminate stray electrical charges that may be induced in the aquarium by the presence of various equipment.

The other is the emergence of enthusiasts for "low-tech" reef tanks that do not employ wet/dry filtration and other forms of technology.

In this respect refer to: "*The Beginner's Guide to Micro and Mini Reef Systems*" by Edward Prasek, recently published by Aardvark Press. I highly recommend it.

• Induced Electrical Charge in the Reef Tank.

In the past few months, much has been learned about the effects of electrical charges in the aquarium. I am not referring here to the charges measured by a redox meter, but rather to the presence of an electrical charge of considerable magnitude that results from induction from nearby electrical equipment.

Now, I frankly do not understand electricity as well as I would like. But, I can wire a lamp, and I understand what is meant by a "ground". If you are with me thus far, keep reading on.

In a marine tank one may have all sorts of electrical equipment: pumps, powerheads, submersible heaters, meters, probes, sterilizers, ozonizers, etc. We can think of this equipment, and especially equipment that is not grounded (usually evidenced by the use of a three-prong plug on the power cord), as capable of "leaking" electricity into the aquarium.

In fact, if one measures, with a voltmeter, the electrical charge on a typical marine tank, one may get a reading of anywhere from zero to perhaps as much as 30 volts.

This fact has been noticed by a number of aquarists. Julian Sprung, writing in the October, 1991 issue of *Freshwater and Marine Aquarium*, not only makes note of this phenomenon, but relates an anecdote wherein the presence of this measurable electrical charge in a marine tank may plausibly have been implicated as a factor in head and lateral line erosion in two species of angelfish. (See *FAMA*, Oct. 1991, page 72.)

Andrew Thomas of Sandpoint Aquarium Products, Eugene Oregon (*personal communication*) discussed electrical charges in the aquarium with me as early as last June, 1991.

It seems that Andrew has investigated this phenomenon extensively, and has had his company manufacture a simple grounding device that, when installed properly in the aquarium, or in the sump of the filter system, permanently and completely solves the problem.

Bruce Davidson, of Sandy's Pet Shop in Louisville, Ken-

tucky, and Hank Diamond, reef enthusiast, also of Louisville, have reported "remarkable" changes in the behavior of both fishes and invertebrates, after grounding
their tanks to eliminate voltages in the 5-30 volt range.

In each case, specimens that tended to be "nervous,
shy, or to hide all the time", no longer exhibited this
behavior, began to feed more avidly and exhibited, in
general, a more healthy appearance.

Omer Dersom, of Energy Savers Unlimited, Torrance,
California, described to me (*personal communication*) the
experiences of several aquarists. Mr. Dersom makes
what are certainly the best aquarium lighting systems
available, and probably knows a thing or two about
electricity.

He relates that customers have sometimes called him to
complain that his light fixtures have given them a mild
shock. This usually occurred when the customer was
simultaneously in contact with the water and the light
fixture. Now, Omer, who really wants to make a good
light fixture, and especially a safe one, knew that his
fixtures were well-grounded, and so could not possibly
be the source of the shock.

So he asked each of these customers to disconnect all
the other equipment on the tank, except the light fixture, and then check to see if they received a mild shock.

As a result of this procedure, every customer found that
the source of the shock was a piece of equipment lacking
a grounded power cord. In other words, the charge in
the tank was traveling from the tank through the
customer's skin, producing the mild shock, and away to
ground by way of the grounded light fixture.

Grounding the tank properly solved this problem, and

Energy Savers's customers have reported, as an unexpected benefit, improvements in the appearance of the tank's inhabitants.

There is ample, although indirect, evidence to suggest that there may be an important biological effect in the aquarium from electrical charges of the magnitude measured and reported by the aquarists just mentioned.

From Andrew Thomas we learn, for example, that studies have shown that the natural electrical charge of the ocean is many, many times smaller than the voltages measured in ungrounded tanks. I remember attending a seminar on sharks that was presented at the 1985 meeting of the American Society of Ichthyologists and Herpetologists.

The shark specialist who presented the seminar compared the electrical sensitivity of certain species of sharks to that of a meter able to detect the electrical potential between two wires connected to opposite poles of a flashlight battery, the other ends of which were separated in the ocean by a distance of two miles!

By comparison to this tiny amount of electricity, the 20 volts or so measured in Mr. Diamond's tank is like the difference between the noise made by a jumbo jet on takeoff and the sound of snowflakes falling on velvet. No wonder fish hide and corals refuse to expand!

Without question, this is an area that deserves further investigation. Fortunately, experiments will be very easy to carry out.

I predict that we shall discover that all marine tanks should be grounded properly to avoid the harmful effects of electrical charges, even minimal ones, on the creatures within the aquarium.

In the meantime, we are testing this hypothesis at Aquatic Specialists, and so far, the results are very positive.

• Low-Tech" Reef Tanks.

Several North American authors most notably, Charles Delbeek and Julian Sprung, are beginning to write about "low-tech" reef tanks in the hobbyist magazines.

I myself first wrote about this subject in the November, 1989 issue of Marine Fish Monthly. In an article entitled, "Reef Tank on a Shoestring", I described a reef aquarium that I had established that did not include a wet/dry filter system.

The key features of my tank are essentially those found in "low-tech" or "natural method" reef tanks around the world.

Such systems have five basic components:

1. Biological filtration and denitrification is accomplished through the use of a large quantity of cured live rock. (See Chapter Four for a discussion of live rock and the curing process.)

2. Chemical filtration is accomplished through the use of a protein skimmer, properly sized to the capacity of the aquarium.

3. Lighting may be either via fluorescent or metal halide lamps, but is always intense, and always chosen to duplicate natural sunlight as closely as possible in terms of spectral distribution.

4. Nothing in the way of organic nutrients is added to the tank, except for occasional feedings for the fish, and

inorganic nutrients are limited by using phosphate- and nitrate-free water and sea salt mixes. Evaporation replacement water is distilled or otherwise purified. Supplements for calcium, and often strontium, molybdenum and iodine are regularly added. Calcium concentration is monitored by testing.

5. Regular partial water changes, siphoning of detritus, and other routine maintenance is carried out, as with any marine tank.

My system has been in operation over two years now, with excellent results.

"Natural" reef tanks are very attractive to hobbyists for a variety of reasons. If carefully planned and executed, these aquariums are in every way as impressive as reef tanks that rely on a variety of technological aids to keep them looking good, at a significant reduction in cost.

Cost savings are typically used to acquire more, or better, specimens of corals, other invertebrates, and fishes. The technique lends itself well to small tanks of ten or twenty gallons, which may be more appropriate for aquarists with limited space.

Perhaps the only drawback to systems of this type is the relatively small numbers of fishes that can be accommodated, since fishes need to be fed (usually three or more times per week), and this makes the task of limiting inorganic nutrients more difficult.

However, most reef enthusiasts agree that invertebrates, not fishes, are the primary focus of reef tanks anyway, and have always limited themselves to a few, smaller species.

Aquarists who desire to create large displays of angelfishes, butterflies, triggers, and wrasses are finding that the wet/dry filter is a better choice for their needs than traditional systems with undergravel filtration.

I predict that the aquarium hobby is moving in the direction of natural systems for tanks that feature invertebrates, and wet/dry systems for tanks that feature fishes.

Assuming that you have decided to establish a natural system reef tank, keep the following points in mind.

1. An external protein skimmer is a must. There are a wide variety of these now on the market, including the recently introduced "Skilter 250" by Eugene Danner Manufacturing Co. This unit combines a traditional "hang-on-the-back" power filter with a small venturi protein skimmer, and will work well on natural system reef tanks up to about 30 gallons. Other external skimmers are available for larger systems.

2. All of the important points about lighting made in Chapter Three apply to natural system tanks, as well.

3. Select the very best quality, fully cured live rock that you can find, for this is a crucial element of the entire system. Live rock that comes from deeper reef areas, encrusted with large amounts of mauve and purple coralline algae, and various small invertebrates, is best.

You will need from one to two pounds of live rock per gallon of tank capacity, depending upon the density of the rock. You need enough to build a structure from about six inches behind the front glass to three-fourths the height of the tank, running the full length of the aquarium.

This structure should be as loosely constructed as possible, with plenty of openings and caves for complete water circulation. There should be no "dead spots" where detritus can accumulate.

4. If the return flow from the skimmer is insufficient to create vigorous water movement throughout most of the tank, add a couple of powerheads to the system to aid in circulation.

Near the front of the tank, in an area that will be easily seen, create a space where water movement is at its lowest point, to accommodate the needs of giant clams, or other invertebrates, that prefer low-current areas.

Any detritus that accumulates in such a location will thus be easily seen and is easily accessible for removal.

5. Automatic evaporation replenishment by means of a float switch is a highly desirable feature of any reef system.

The evaporation replenishment equipment may also be used to dispense inorganic supplements, such as calcium, strontium, etc., on a programmed basis.

Natural systems are not really new, by the way. I have an old copy of the *TFH* (*Tropical Fish Hobbyist*) classic *Exotic Marine Fishes*, in which reference is made to an Indonesian aquarist who used only live rock and an airstone to create beautiful invertebrate displays back in the 1950's! Checking around you can probably find such picutres yourself.

In all cases, reef tanks established by the natural method need the same testing, maintenance and attention to the biological needs of the inhabitants in order to flourish. But, because of their greater simplicity, these systems are proving themselves to be easy to maintain.

I strongly advocate the continuation of interest in natural reef aquariums.

Refer to E. Prasek's book mentioned earlier. It will prove a wise decision for you to read it especially since all you will need to set up such an aquarium is 2 canister filters and a protein skimmer!

I hope that hobbyists who formerly spent time learning about high-tech equipment will now have time to learn about the biological needs of the invertebrates, macro-algae and fishes.

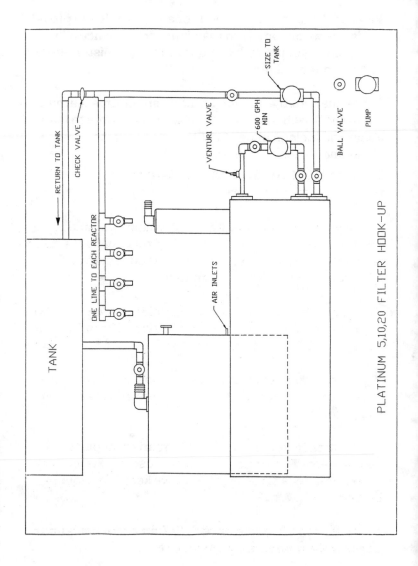

PLATINUM 5,10,20 FILTER HOOK-UP

Appendices

Understanding Scientific Names

Many people seem to find scientific names daunting. I have a little trouble understanding this, since we use terms like "Chrysanthemum" and "Rhododendron" and "Philodendron" without hesitation.

Why are the scientific names for plants easy for the average person to use, but not the scientific names for aquarium fishes and invertebrates?

Perhaps I shall never know the reason for this anomalous situation. However, I would like to make an attempt to change it.

If aquarists in general, and reef aquarists in particular, would become more fluent in the use of the correct scientific names of the organisms we keep, we would all be better off. Why?

Because scientific names make all of our communications about these organisms more precise.

The species that I refer to as Flowerpot Coral may be called Sunflower Coral where you come from, but the scientific name *Goniopora lobata* is unambiguous and leaves no doubt as to which coral one is referring to.

This is the beauty of scientific names, every organism that has been formally described by a biologist has but one scientific name, and this name is used throughout the world to refer to this particular organism.

So whether you are in Bangkok or Boise, *Goniopora lobata* refers to the same animal — "Flowerpot Coral" could mean something different, depending upon local usage.

As aquarists gain more experience with maintaining marine fish and invertebrates in their aquariums, and share their observations with each other, the importance of having a precise understanding about just which organism is being discussed can hardly be overestimated.

Many times a particular species that is easy to keep has a relative that is similar in appearance, but is very difficult to keep. Confusion can easily arise when only common names are used in reference to these organisms.

Apart from the elimination of confusion in discussions of aquarium husbandry and so forth, scientific names can, if understood, supply valuable information about the organisms to which they refer.

Most scientific names mean something.

Consider the Green Sea Mat, *Zoanthus sociatus*. Loosely translated this means "flower animal that lives in colonies." Or the Longnosed Butterflyfish, *Forcipiger flavissimus*, whose name means "the most yellow forceps-carrier". Isn't this fun?

Each scientific name consits of two parts. The first part identifies the genus (plural, genera) or group, to which the organism belongs. Thus, *Forcipiger flavissimus* and *Forcipiger longirostris* are two species within the same genus.

The second part of the name identifies the species. *F. longirostris* is thus "the long-snouted forceps-carrier". And, indeed, the snout of this butterflyfish is much longer than that of the "Longnosed Butterflyfish", *F. flavissimus*. See how confusing common names can be?

Taken together, the two parts of the scientific name uniquely identify a specific organism.

Several rules apply to the use of scientific names:

1. The genus name can stand alone to represent all members of the genus, e.g., *Caulerpa*. However, the species name can never stand alone. For example, "*flavissimus*", by itself, is meaningless.

2. Scientific names are always italicized.

3. When a list of species within a single genus is being presented, the generic name is spelled out the first time it is used. Thereafter, it may be abbreviated, as in "*Forcipiger flavissimus*, and its cousin, *F. longirostris*, both occur in the Indo-Pacific."

4. Biologists group genera to form families. Family groupings are often convenient for the aquarist, since members of a given family frequently share similar traits. Family names are capitalized, but not italicized, and always end in "**idae**".

The family name is generally taken from the generic name of the most common or best known member of the family. Thus, all the butterflyfish family is "*Chaeto-dontidae*", from *Chaetodon*, the genus to which most butterflyfishes are assigned.

Forcipiger belongs to this family, along with *Chelmon*, *Chelmonops*, *Coradion*, and *Hemitaurichthys*, all various genera of butterflyfishes.

Several conventional methods are used by biologists to create scientific names. Knowledge of these may help the aquarist in understanding something about the organism bearing the name, and may in some cases, make the pronunciation of the name easier.

Often an organism is named in honor of a person. In this case the species name ends in "i" if the honoree was male, or "ae" if the honoree was female.

Periclimenes pedersoni, thus, is the name for Pederson's Cleaning Shrimp. The "i" always carries the long vowel sound, i.e., "PEE-der-sun-eye" in this example, and the "ae" ending is always pronounced as a long "e", as in *Allomicrodesmis dorotheae*, "Dorothy's fish that is similar to Microdesmis". The species name is pronounced "door-o-THE-ee".

The place where the species occurs may be used in the name, and this is usually indicated by the ending "ensis". The species *Pomachromis guamensis*, therefore, is found around Guam, and this name is pronounced "GUAM-in-sis."

Scientific names are used throughout this book, in the hope that they will become more familiar to aquarists. Practice using scientific names; they are a precise and meaningful way to refer to the organisms we keep in our aquariums.

Abbreviations

Abbreviations used in this book are listed below:

DO	dissolved oxygen
DOC	dissolved organic carbon
K	Kelvin temperature
KH	carbonate hardness (German)
meq/l	milliequivalents per liter
mg/l	milligrams per liter
ml	milliliter(s)
mV	millivolts
ppb	parts per billion
ppm	parts per million
UV	ultraviolet
o/oo	parts per thousand
F°	Fahrenheit degrees
C°	Celsius degrees

Trademarks and Brands

Following is a list of trademarks and brand names used in this book, together with the name of the company that owns the trademark or manufactures the brand of product listed.

Coralife™ is a registered trademark of Energy Savers Unlimited, Inc., Torrance, CA.

Lifeguard™ is a registered trademark of Rainbow Plastics, El Monte, CA.

Marineland Magnum 330 filter is manufactured by Marineland Aquarium Products, A Division of Aquaria, Inc., Simi Valley, CA.

Poly-Filter™ is a registered trademark of Poly-Bio Marine, Inc., South Orange, NJ.

X-Nitrate, X-Phosphate, Liquid Gold, SuperTechs, Redox+ and others are products of Thiel-Aqua-Tech Inc., Las Cruces, NM.

Roti-Rich is a product of Florida Aqua Farms, Dade City, Florida

Selcon™ is a registered trademark of American Marine, Ridgefield, CT.

Vita-Boost™ is a registered trademark of Ocean Nutrition, National City, CA.

Vita-Chem is a product of Boyd Enterprises, Miami, FL.

Trademarks are strongly protected by Federal Law and the small ™ after a product name refers specifically to that protection.

Bibliography

Bold, H.C. and M.J. Wynne. (1978) Introduction to the Algae. Prentice-Hall, Inc., Englewood Cliffs, NJ. 706 pp.

Colin, P.I. (1978) Caribbean Reef Invertebrates and Plants. TFH Publications, Inc., Neptune City, NJ. 512 pp.

Debelius, H. (1989) Fishes for the Invertebrate Aquarium, 3rd ed. Aquarium Systems, Inc., Mentor, OH. 160 pp.

Devaney, D.M. and L.G. Eldridge, eds. (1977) Reef and Shore Fauna of Hawaii Section I: Protozoa through Ctenophora. Bishop Museum Press, Honolulu, HI. 278 pp.

_____ (1987) Reef and Shore Fauna of Hawaii Section 2: Platyhelminthes through Phoronida and Section 3: Sipuncula through Annelida. Bishop Museum Press, Honolulu, HI. 461 pp.

George, J.D. and J.J. George. (1979) Marine Life: An Illustrated Encyclopedia of Invertebrates in the Sea. John Wiley and Sons, New York. 288 pp.

Kaplan, E.H. (1982) A Field Guide to Coral Reefs of the Caribbean and Florida. Houghton Mifflin Company, Boston. 289 pp.

Kerstitch, A. (1989) Sea of Cortez Marine Invertebrates: A Guide for the Pacific Coast, Mexico to Ecuador. Sea Challengers, Monterrey, CA. 114 pp.

Moe, M. (1989) Marine Aquarium Reference: Systems and Invertebrates. Green Turtle Publications, Plantation Key, Fl. 507 pp.

Myers, R.F. (1989) Micronesian Reef Fishes. Coral Graphics, Guam. 298 pp.

Prasek, E.D. (1992) The Beginner's Guide to Micro and Mini Reef Systems. Aardvark Press. 72 pp.

Roessler, C. (undated) The Underwater Wilderness. Chanticleer Press, Inc., New York. 319 pp.

Spotte, S. (1979) Seawater Aquariums. John Wiley and Sons, Inc., New York. 413 pp.

Sterrer, W. (1986) Marine Flora and Fauna of Bermuda. John Wiley and Sons, Inc., New York. 742 pp.

Taylor, W.R. (1960) Marine Algae of the Eastern Tropical and Subtropical Coasts of the Americas. University of Michigan Press, Ann Arbor. 870 pp.

Thiel, A.J. (1988) The Marine Fish and Invert Reef Aquarium. Aardvark Press, Las Cruces NM. 319 pp.
_____ (1989) Advanced Reef Keeping. Aardvark Press, Las Cruces, NM. 440 pp.
_____ (1992) Ten Easy Steps to a great looking saltwater aquarium. Aardvark Press, Las Cruces, NM. 192 pp
_____ (1991) Small Reef Aquarium Basics, Aardvark Press, Las Cruces, NM. 176 pp.

Thomson, D.A., L.T. Findley and A. Kerstitch. (1979) Reef Fishes of the Sea of Cortez. University of Arizona Press, Tuscon. 302 pp.

Veron, J.E.N. (1986) Corals of Australia and the Indo-Pacific. Angus and Robertson Publishers, North Ryde, Australia. 644 pp.

Walls, J.G., ed. (1982) Encyclopedia of Marine Invertebrates. TFH Publications, Inc., Neptune City, New Jersey. 736 pp.

Wood, E.M. (1983) Corals of the World. TFH Publications, Inc., Neptune City, New Jersey. 256 pp.

Zann, L.P. (1988) Marine Community Aquarium. TFH Publications, Inc., Neptune City, New Jersey. 416 pp.

Index

C

H

I

For those interested the index was created using Nisus 3.06 Wordprocessing.

Aardvark Press

also publishes the

following books :

* The Marine Fish and Invert Reef Aquarium

   * Ten Easy Steps to a Great Looking
        Saltwater Aquarium

      * Advanced Reef Keeping I

   * The Marine Reef Harbound Version
   (34 issues of t he newsletter 467 pp.)

      * and the soon to be released
Advanced Reef Keeping II, The Invertebrates

all the above books are written

by Albert J. Thiel

Products mentioned in this book are
available form dealers nationwide

Call Aardvark Press or
Aquatic Specialists in
Knoxville, Tennessee
for more details.

We encourage you to send us
feedback on this book so
we may incorporate possible
improvements in future
printings. Thank You.